IRELAND'S
ROUND TOWERS

IRELAND'S
ROUND TOWERS

BUILDINGS, RITUALS AND LANDSCAPES
OF THE EARLY IRISH CHURCH

Tadhg O'Keeffe

TEMPUS

First published 2004

Tempus Publishing Ltd
The Mill, Brimscombe Port
Stroud, Gloucestershire GL5 2QG
www.tempus-publishing.com

British Library Cataloguing in Publication Data.
A catalogue record for this book is available from the British Library.

ISBN 0 7524 2571 4

Typesetting and origination by Tempus Publishing.
Printed and bound in Great Britain.

Contents

List of illustrations

Figures in text

Colour plates

Preface

Few monuments in the Irish countryside fascinate us as Round Towers do. Few are as treasured, as witnessed by the fact that most of the surviving examples are in state care. Few are scrutinised so carefully by modern visitors, and yet few are so rarely entered by those same visitors. Round Towers are among the most enigmatic of medieval buildings anywhere. This book is intended as a visitor-friendly guide to these remarkable relics of the medieval Irish Church.

The literature on Ireland's Round Towers is fairly extensive. A perusal of the most recent writings will indicate that the dates and functions of the towers are fairly well established. There is general agreement that the main period of their construction was between the start of the tenth century and the end of the twelfth century. There is also agreement that they were, first and foremost, the bell-houses of church sites. The authorities for such an interpretation are as good as they come: the medieval annalists or chroniclers on whom we depend so heavily for information about earlier medieval Ireland actually *tell us* that these were bell-houses. There is also general agreement that Round Towers functioned as symbols of the wealth of monasteries, that they were occasion-ally treasuries in which relics and other valuables were stored, and that they were occasionally used (and maybe even designed to be used) as places of refuge when communities were attacked. So, more than a century and a half after the first serious scholarly research on these marvellous buildings was published, we seem to have arrived at a consensus.

The idea of writing a small, popular book about Round Towers for a general readership came to me in 1999. Accompanied by my colleagues and good friends, Mick Aston and Mark Horton, I brought a small group of archaeology students from University College Dublin and the University of Bristol to see the monastic complex of Kilmacduagh and talked to them about that site's Round Tower, filling in possible missing bits of that particular tower's history with anecdotes drawn from annalistic records of other towers, and explaining its general architectural context by pointing to the other buildings in the fields around it. This book began, there and then, with the idea of presenting in print what is essentially a very long field trip (or even classroom) lecture, integrating explanations of different aspects of the towers and of the sites on which they are found, and stressing just how important these buildings are in the history of Irish, and indeed European, architecture. This book's chatty style derives from these circumstances of its conception, as does its lack of the normal scholarly apparatus of the footnote or bibliographic reference. Its anticipated readership comprises people who would like to hear an explanation whispered in their ear as they stand – often in the cold! – looking up at one of these great towers. So, where I cite certain features as common or uncommon but without giving supporting evidence, or offer dates which seem quite specific, again without chapter and verse, I request that the reader simply trusts me! And I hope that colleagues familiar with Irish architectural history will automatically know the basis for any unsupported statement.

Kite-flying is one of the joys of lecturing, and Round Towers lend themselves easily to it. But there are kites and there are kites! For as long as people have been thinking about these monuments they have been thinking rather silly things about them. Round Towers have been identified as temples of pagan sun-worship, fire-worship and phallus-worship, as astronomical observatories, as nodal points on ley lines which also run underneath Egyptian pyramids, and so on. At the same time, the scholarly community, aware perhaps that Round Towers and such 'fringe' interpretations have always seemed to go hand-in-hand, may have clamped its own historical imagination when dealing with these buildings. Having seen off a raft of explanations ranging from the amusingly imaginative to the certifiably bonkers, scholars are happy to leave the perfectly reasonable modern consensus about the towers exactly where it is.

But the very admission that these are extraordinary buildings should keep us thinking about them. Here are some pointers:

First, their unmistakable physical presence contrasts with the small and unimposing character of the other early medieval buildings associated with them, including the most sacred buildings of all, the churches. The towers' masons rose to the technical challenges of tower-construction with considerable zeal, sometimes even dressing the stones to have curved surfaces, and yet they seem to have remained oblivious to the challenge of building larger churches, or of building small churches with greater finesse.

Secondly, in some instances, and maybe in every instance, royal money was spent on the towers. Knowing the general nature of medieval architectural patronage, one is struck by the notion of a king providing patronage for a bell-house when, under its shadow, is a modest church in which his munificence might find a more conventional outlet.

Thirdly, what about deaths in Round Towers? These buildings are sometimes recorded as having been places of violent death, often of large numbers of people, and yet they were singularly ill-equipped for the protection or self-defence of their occupants in times of trouble. More interestingly, some of the recorded fatalities are of people – kings, specifically – whom one would not expect to find inside a bell-house, even in the most trying of circumstances.

Clearly there is more to these buildings than meets the eye, and we need to look a little beyond the annalists' miserly hints – though perhaps not as far beyond as sun-worship! – in searching for it.

The definitive book on the Irish Round Tower, if such a thing can be envisaged for any topic, will need to draw on full architectural surveys of the buildings as well as on historical surveys of the sites that they occupy. And it will need also to cross-reference with the research outcomes of many fields. My ambitions for this present book, beyond revealing their place in Irish architectural history to their modern visitors, is to suggest to readers (including colleagues, in my own field of archaeology as well as in other areas of scholarship) that the towers demand that very detailed level of cross-disciplinary enquiry, and that our understanding of medieval Ireland will profit greatly from it. Round Towers are not marginalia in the history of Ireland; they a central part of the story. I *want* this book to open up discussion of them again.

This book has three parts. The first, comprising the first two chapters, presents some of the basic facts about tower history, architecture and chronology. The second, consisting of the third and fourth chapters, is more analytical, exploring what the towers were for and where the ideas came from. The final part is intended to make this a useful book to have in the car's glove compartment – a short summary of the surviving towers. More extensive accounts are available in print but in forms that are sometimes unwieldy when traipsing around fields.

This work was originally planned for publication in a new series under the general editorship of Professor David Dumville of the University of Cambridge, but the illustrative requirements eventually made that an impractical option. I am grateful to Peter Kemmis Betty for taking it on at Tempus, and to Emma Parkin for seeing it through production. I would like to express my gratitude to Dr Jane Hawkes, now of the University of York, for supportive comments at a crucial moment in its gestation, to Dr Ailbhe MacShamhráin, of the National University of Ireland, Maynooth, for helpful comments on the text, and to my old friend Christy Roche in Fermoy, Co. Cork, who allowed me to rifle through his photograph collection for images. The nicest ones here are probably his!

1
Annalists, antiquarians, nationalists
Round Towers in history

The Ireland of early Christianity is popularly described as the land of saints and scholars. It is a phrase that captures nicely the traditional understanding that those most virtuous of qualities – holiness and scholarship – were possessed by many among the island's inhabitants a thousand years ago. That ancient Ireland should be remembered as a theatre of piety and learning, as a place where wholesome Celtic values co-existed with the purist of apostolic virtues, and in settings of unsurpassed beauty (**2**), is intrinsically interesting. A strange mélange of myth and fact, this half-truth – yes, there *were* saints and scholars, but there were many others besides, and it is a moot point whether any them should be called 'Celts' – found its way to the centre of Irish national identity as it emerged in the nineteenth and early twentieth centuries. The remarkable monuments and objects of Ireland's Christian past, such as High Crosses and illuminated gospel books, were singled out as both beacons of this rich and ancient heritage and symbols of its enduring relevance. The Round Tower, a truly nationwide phenomenon (**1**), was arguably the most potent, the most iconic, among these inanimate symbols of 'Irishness'. This judgement is based less on its appearance within a panoply of symbolic motifs on public houses (**3**) than on its selection for the 1869 monument in Glasnevin cemetery in Dublin which commemorates Daniel O'Connell, the Kerryman whose greatest political achievement was to secure emancipation for Irish Catholics in 1829 (**4**).

The testimony of the annalists

What do medieval voices tell us about Round Towers? The answer is: much less than we would like. Medieval Irish chroniclers – the authors and compilers of those annals which constitute our basic historical source material for medieval Gaelic Ireland – made reference to a Round Tower only when they felt the recording of some incident or event involving a tower was warranted.

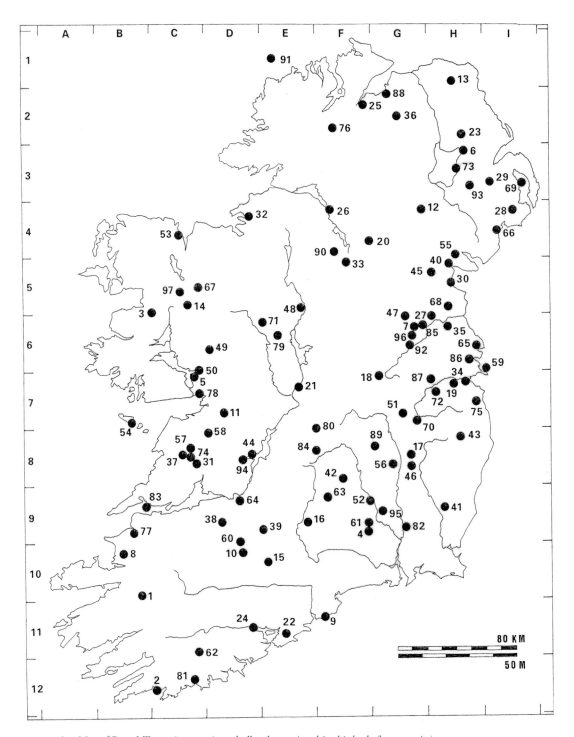

1 *Map of Round Tower sites, certain and alleged, mentioned in this book (key opposite)*

1 Aghadoe, Co. Kerry [B10]
2 Aghadown, Co. Cork [C12]
3 Aghagower, Co. Mayo [C5]
4 Aghaviller, Co. Kilkenny [F9]
5 Annaghdown. Co. Galway [C7]
6 Antrim, Co. Antrim [H3]
7 Ardbraccan, Co. Meath [G6]
8 Ardfert, Co. Kerry [B10]
9 Ardmore, Co. Waterford [F11]
10 Ardpatrick, Co. Limerick [D10]
11 Ardrahan, Co. Galway [D7]
12 Armagh, Co. Armagh [G4]
13 Armoy, Co. Antrim [H1]
14 Balla, Co. Mayo [C5]
15 Brigown, Co. Cork [E10]
16 Cashel, Co, Tipperary [E9]
17 Castledermot, Co. Kildare [G8]
18 Clonard, Co. Meath [G7]
19 Clondalkin, Co. Dublin [H7]
20 Clones, Co. Monaghan [F4]
21 Clonmacnoise, Co. Offaly [E7]
22 Cloyne, Co. Cork [E11]
23 Connor, Co. Antrim [H2]
24 Cork, Co. Cork [D11]
25 Derry, Co. Derry [F2]
26 Devenish, Co. Fermanagh [F4]
27 Donaghmore, Co. Meath [G6]
28 Downpatrick, Co. Down [I4]
29 Drumbo, Co. Antrim [I3]
30 Dromiskin, Co. Louth [H5]
31 Drumcliff, Co. Clare [C8]
32 Drumcliff, Co. Sligo [D4]
33 Drumlane, Co. Cavan [F5]
34 Dublin – St Michael-le-Pole [H7]
35 Duleek, Co. Meath [H6]
36 Dungiven, Co. Derry [G2]
37 Dysert O'Dea, Co. Clare [C8]
38 Dysert Oenghusa, Co. Limerick [D9]
39 Emly, Co. Tipperary [D9]
40 Faughart, Co. Louth [H5]
41 Ferns, Co. Wexford [H9]
42 Fertagh, Co. Kilkenny [F8]
43 Glendalough, Co. Wicklow [H8]
44 Inis Cealtra, Co. Clare [D8]
45 Inishkeen, Co. Monaghan [H50]
46 Kellistown, Co. Carlow [G8]
47 Kells, Co. Meath [G6]
48 Kilbarry, Co. Roscommon [E5]
49 Kilbennan, Co. Galway [C6]

50 Kilcoona, Co. Galway [C6]
51 Kildare, Co. Kildare [G7]
52 Kilkenny Co. Kilkenny [F9]
53 Killala, Co. Mayo [C4]
54 Killeany, Co. Galway [B7]
55 Killeevy, Co. Armagh [H4]
56 Killeshin, Co. Laois [G8]
57 Killinaboy, Co. Clare [C8]
58 Kilmacduagh, Co. Galway [D8]
59 Kilmacnessan, Co. Dublin [H6]
60 Kilmallock, Co. Limerick [D9]
61 Kilree, Co. Kilkenny [F9]
62 Kinneigh, Co. Cork [C11]
63 Liathmore, Co. Tipperary [F9]
64 Limerick, Co. Limerick [D9]
65 Lusk, Co. Dublin [H6]
66 Maghera, Co. Down [I4]
67 Meelick, Co. Mayo [C5]
68 Monasterboice, Co. Louth [H5]
69 Nendrum, Co. Down [I3]
70 Old Kilcullen, Co. Kildare [G7]
71 Oran, Co. Roscommon [E6]
72 Oughterard, Co. Kildare [H7]
73 Ram's Island, Co. Antrim [H3]
74 Rath Blathmac, Co. Clare [C8]
75 Rathmichael, Co. Dublin [H7]
76 Raphoe, Co. Donegal [F2]
77 Rattoo, Co. Kerry [B9]
78 Roscam, Co. Galway [C7]
79 Roscommon, Co. Roscommon [F6]
80 Roscrea, Co. Tipperary [E8]
81 Ross Carbery, Co. Cork [C12]
82 St Mullins, Co. Carlow [G9]
83 Scattery Island, Co. Clare [B9]
84 Seir Kieran, Co. Offaly [F8]
85 Slane, Co. Meath [G6]
86 Swords, Co. Dublin [H6]
87 Taghadoe, Co. Kildare [G7]
88 Tamlaght, Co. Derry [G2]
89 Timahoe, Co. Laois [F80
90 Tomregan, Co. Cavan [F4]
91 Tory Island, Co. Donegal [E1]
92 Trim, Co. Meath [G6]
93 Trummery, Co. Antrim [H3]
94 Tuamgraney, Co. Clare [D8]
95 Tullaherin, Co. Kilkenny [F9]
96 Tullaghard, Co. Meath [G6]
97 Turlough, Co. Mayo [C5]

2 *St Kevin's church at Glendalough, in verdant surrounds and overlooked by steep, forested, slopes*

Listed below are the twenty-five annalistic references to towers, located at twenty-two places, which means that there is no documentation in more than half-a-dozen or so annalistic compilations for more than two-thirds of the known Round Towers. So, there is no hint in their records that annalists regarded these buildings as exceptional in any way, or that they would have expected later generations to venerate them as symbolic of the Christian world which created them. They may have found the towers as fascinating as we do, but it was not their job to express such thoughts. Consequently, they recorded the destruction of towers far more frequently than they recorded their construction.

The annalists' preferred word for a tower was *cloicthe[a]ch*, literally 'bell-house'. They sometimes made specific reference to a tower's cap, using the word *bennchobbor/bennchobhar*; on rare occasions they may have used this as a synonym for *cloictheach*. Needless to say, Round Tower is a relatively modern couplet, in widespread use since at least the early 1800s.

3   *The pediment of a late nineteenth-century public house in Ringsend, Dublin*

The following is a list of the events in which Round Towers are either impli-
cated or mentioned in passing in surviving annalistic sources (see the List of
abbreviations, p.155). There are slight discrepancies in date between the annals
with respect to individual events; generally the date as given in the *Annals of
Ulster* is given preference here.

950   Slane, Co. Meath
The Round Tower is burned by Vikings ('foreigners'). It was full of relics,
including the crosier of the patron saint, a bell ('the best of bells'), and 'distinguished persons', including the lector (*ferleigind*) of Slane (AClon 945; CS 949;
AFM 948; AU 950).

964   Tuamgraney, Co. Clare
Cormac Ua Cillin, *comarb* and bishop of Tuamgraney, dies in this year, and his
obituary records that he had built the 'great' church and Round Tower of
Tuamgraney (CS 964).

981   Louth
Stormy weather is blamed for the collapse of many 'steeples' (taken to mean
Round Towers), of which that at Louth, which 'fell down violently', is the
only one named. This record survives in the so-called *Annals of Clonmacnoise*,

4 *The Daniel O'Connell memorial in Glasnevin cemetery, Dublin*

a problematic seventeenth-century copy of a lost annalistic source. The *Annals of the Four Masters*, a far more reliable compilation of the same general date, makes no reference to a Round Tower at Louth but mentions the loss of a timber church in 986, so there is some doubt about this reference (AClon 981).

996 Armagh

Lightning burns the settlement of Armagh, including, according to most sources, its stone church and Round Tower. One source uses the term *benn-chobbor*, suggesting it is the top of the tower that is hit, while another indicates more than one tower is burned (AClon 994; CS 994; AT, AFM 995; AI 996).

1015/6 Downpatrick, Co. Down

Lightning burns Downpatrick, including its stone church and Round Tower (AFM 1015).

1020 Armagh

A fire of unspecified cause is recorded as destroying Armagh, including its stone churches and its Round Tower 'with all its bells'. This is a major and extensive fire indeed: all the annals which have records for 1020 – a couple of the compilations have gaps at this time – mention it (AClon 1013; CS 1018; AU, ALC, AT, AI, AFM 1020).

1039 Clonard, Co. Meath

The Round Tower falls down, but no cause is given (AClon, AFM 1039).

1050 Roscommon

The Round Tower is burned by the men of Breifne (AFM 1050).

1058 Emly, Co. Tipperary

The Round Tower and stone church at Emly are 'totally burned' but the circumstances are not specified (AU, ALC, AFM 1058).

1076 Kells, Co. Meath

The new king of Tara, Murchad, son of Flann Ua Maeleachlainn, is murdered in the tower at Kells by the lord of Gailenga, Amhlaeibh, only three days into his reign (**5**; CS 1073; AClon 1075; AU, ALC, AT, AI, AFM 1076).

1097 Monasterboice, Co. Louth

The Round Tower, the books and the 'many treasures' within it are burned, though in circumstances that are unrecorded (**colour plate 1**; CS 1093; AU, AFM 1097).

5 *The Round Tower at Kells with an unfinished (tenth-century?) High Cross in the foreground*

6 *Tullaherin Round Tower under modern scaffolding. The top of the tower was rebuilt in the late Middle Ages*

1121 Armagh
The cap (*benncobbar*) of the Round Tower is knocked off by a strong wind which also felled woods throughout Ireland (AU, ALC, AFM 1121).

1121 Tullaherin, Co, Kilkenny
The Round Tower at *Telach Innmuin* (sometimes identified as Tullamaine but actually Tullaherin) is struck and split by a 'thunderbolt'; a stone flies into the church and kills a student (**6**; AU, ALC, AFM 1121).

1124 Clonmacnoise, Co. Offaly
The completion of the Round Tower by Abbot Gilla Chríst Ó Máeleoin, supported by Toirrdelbach Ó Conchobhair, king of Connacht, is recorded (**colour plate 2**; CS 1120; AFM 1124).

1126/7   Trim, Co. Meath
A northern army burns the church and Round Tower in Trim, both of them full of people. The *Annals of Innisfallen*, a chronicle written in Munster, places the attack in 1128 and makes no reference to the Round Tower (MIA 1126/7).

1130-1   Drumbo, Co. Down
An army from central and western Ulster (modern Tyrone and Donegal) attacks Ulaid (modern eastern Ulster), and plunders the Round Tower and timber church at Drumbo, stealing books from the latter (MIA 1130-1).

1135   Clonmacnoise, Co. Offaly
Lightning hits the top of the Round Tower at Clonmacnoise (CS 1131; AFM 1135).

1135   Roscrea, Co. Tipperary
Lightning 'pierces' the Round Tower of Roscrea (**7**; CS 1131; AFM 1135).

1147   Duleek, Co. Meath
A 'thunderbolt' knocks the cap off this tower (**colour plate 3**; AFM 1147)

1156   Fertagh, Co. Kilkenny
One source records the burning during war of the Round Tower at Aghmacart, Co. Laois, and the death of the lector (*fer leghínd*) inside it, and another records the death of the 'chief master' (*ardmhaighistor*) in the tower at Fertagh, which is near Aghmacart. Both events are one and the same, and the tower at Fertagh is the site (**8**; AT, AFM 1156).

1171   Tullaghard, Co. Meath
The Round Tower at Tullaghard (Tullyard) is attacked and burned 'with its full of people' by an army from Breifne (AT, AFM 1171).

1176   Devenish, Co. Fermanagh
The king of Fir Manach is burned by his kinsmen in the Round Tower here (**colour plate 4**; MIA 1176).

1181   Ardbraccan, Co. Meath
The Round Tower falls down; the reason is not specified (AClon 1181).

1238   Annaghdown, Co. Galway
This Round Tower is built (ALC, AFM 1238).

7 Left *The Round Tower at Roscrea*

8 Right *The Round Tower at Fertagh*

Let us summarise this information; a more thorough analysis of what it tells us about the functions of the towers will be offered in chapter 3.

We have just three references to tower construction. The earliest is that indirect reference to the now-lost tower at Tuamgraney. The death in 964 of the churchman under whom it was built allows us to place its construction in the middle of the tenth century. The second reference, which is to Clonmacnoise's tower in 1124, is especially valuable, in part because it illuminates the co-operation of a king and a senior cleric in the building of a tower, and in part because the building in question still stands. The third reference is perhaps the most fascinating. It is to the building of a tower at Annaghdown in 1238. This is very late indeed: the latest that one can date any of the extant towers stylistically is the mid-1100s (in the case of Timahoe), or maybe, as some writers would hold, the later 1100s (in the case of Ardmore). The annalists passed no remark on Annaghdown, but the very fact that they recorded it at all when they blithely ignored other acts of construction suggests that it interested them. We will return to it later.

In most instances, as we noted, the annalistic references to Round Towers are to their partial or complete destruction. In a few instances no explanation is given. One suspects that natural, non-violent, factors – lightning, big winds, simple mechanical failure – caused destruction of most of those towers for which no information other than destruction was recorded. The towers of Clonard and Ardbraccan are recorded as having simply fallen down in 1039 and 1181 respectively; natural forces may have weakened them over time or perhaps they had slow-burn structural faults. Lightning or big winds are explicitly blamed in the cases of the destruction of the towers of Louth and unnamed other places in 981, Armagh in 996 and again in 1121, Downpatrick in 1015 or 1016, Tullaherin in 1121, Clonmacnoise and Roscrea in 1135, and Duleek in 1147. The seventeenth-century *Annals of Clonmacnoise*, copied from now-lost earlier sources, record the blowing down in strong winds of many 'steeples' – Round Towers – in 1137. Later annals tell us that a Round Tower at Rosscarbery was blown down by strong winds in 1285 and that the tower at Drumcliff in Sligo (**9**) was struck by lightning in 1396. Destruction is attributed to acts of violence in the cases of Slane in 950, Roscommon in 1050, Trim in 1126 or 1127, Fertagh in 1156, and Tullaghard in 1171. In each of these instances there was an actual attack on the tower, and fatalities are recorded at Slane, Trim, Fertagh and Tullaghard. Blame is popularly apportioned to Vikings, but Slane is the only place where the blame is correctly targeted; in most cases the perpetrators were Irish. The tower at Drumbo was plundered in 1130 or 1131 but was not damaged, or at least not damaged enough for annalists to take note.

Incidentally, many other towers display some external evidence of having been burned in circumstances not recorded. Burning timber buildings might have fallen against them, thereby causing accidental and somewhat localised

9   Above *The Round Tower at Drumcliff (Sligo)*

10   Below *A medieval conflagration unknown to the annalists? Fire-damaged stones at the base of Meelick Round Tower*

11 *The doorway of Aghagower Round Tower displays evidence of a fire of considerable intensity*

damage to the tower fabric, as may be the case at Meelick (**10**), but in most cases the likelihood is that they were deliberately set on fire (with bonfires set at their bases) in undocumented episodes of violence or acts of vandalism. The shattered surfaces of the stones on the doorway of the Aghagower tower indicate a well-fuelled fire (**11**). These might not have been medieval conflagrations; given the obvious dangers of demolishing a Round Tower by quarrying its base, people over the centuries may have tried to demolish towers by setting fires at their bases.

The annals tell us a little about the buildings accompanying the towers. Stone churches are mentioned at Armagh in 996 and 1020, at Downpatrick in 1015 or 1016, and at Emly in 1058, but a timber church or oratory (*duirrtheac*) was plundered along with the tower at Drumbo.

12   *The base of a possible Round Tower at Faughart*

Other sources – a brief comment

Antiquarian records from the eighteenth and nineteenth centuries tell us of other towers, undocumented in the Middle Ages and now lost. Seven towers have such good antiquarian records that their former existence is beyond question: Brigown, Cork, Derry, Kilbarry, Killeshin, Raphoe and Rath Blathmac. A further four identifications – Aghadown, Connor, Kellistown and Limerick – are based on moderately reliable antiquarian sources or local traditions.

Needless to say, the field evidence is our principal source, and as it provides the basis for most of this book only a brief comment is needed here. Despite the fact that some towers barely survive above foundation level, there are only two suggested Round Tower identifications 'in the field' that might be queried. One of these is at Faughart. The ring of stones that is taken to be the remains of a destroyed tower (**12**) certainly has the correct dimensions for one, as well as an offset at ground level of a type that is commonly found on towers. Moreover, it is in an area where Round Towers are not uncommon. Considering the appearance of the base of a destroyed tower (discovered by good fortune when a fence was being made in 1973) at Devenish (**colour plate 4**, *bottom*) and the similar foundation (discovered in excavations by Robin Glasscock in 1969) at Liathmore (**13**), the Faughart monument has the appearance of a deliberately preserved Round Tower base. It must be conceded, though, that the presence of a High Cross base in the centre of the ring of stones, and of an upright stone at the edge of the ring, suggest that this foundation may be a form of *leacht* or altar rather than part of a Round Tower. The other example that might be disputed is the cylindrical tower in the west façade of the collegiate church in Kilmallock (**14**). The fabric is inconclusive, but its form and setting are unusual enough for it to be regarded as a probable rather than a possible Round Tower.

A history of Round Tower research

Having examined what contemporary medieval annalists had to say about Round Towers, let us look now at the endeavours of the first scholars in the nineteenth century to make sense of these enigmatic buildings.

The O'Connell monument, mentioned above, was designed by George Petrie, a landscape painter, a collector of music and an antiquarian, who had worked as a professional scholar with the Ordnance Survey and was a long-time member of the Royal Irish Academy. Petrie was a distinguished scholar, and his name is one of the few from that period to be familiar to all modern archaeologists in Ireland.

Petrie was the acknowledged authority on these towers around the time of O'Connell's death in 1847. Back in 1830, in his capacity as a member of its Committee of Antiquities, he had suggested to the Royal Irish Academy that

13 *The excavated Round Tower base at Liathmore*

14 *A possible Round Tower incorporated into the west end of the (thirteenth- and fifteenth-century) collegiate church of SS Peter and Paul at Kilmallock. The upper parts are certainly late medieval*

they make the origin and use of the Round Tower the subject of a prize essay. They did, and he went on to win it himself! It was, in fairness to him, a topic that exercised learned minds at that time, and he was certainly a deserving winner.

George Petrie and the phallic symbols

The fundamental argument of the essay with which Petrie won the Academy's prize of a gold medal and fifty guineas was that the towers were indisputably products of Christian culture, as some earlier writers had indeed suggested. Obvious though this theory seems now, there was a strongly-held view in the later eighteenth and early nineteenth centuries, even within the Academy, that ancient Ireland had fallen under the influence of pagan Phoenicians and that the towers, notwithstanding the Christian gravestones rising all around them (**15** and **colour plate 5**), had been places of Phoenician fire-worship. Petrie's rival for the Academy prize was one Henry O'Brien, a graduate of Trinity College Dublin, whose essay offered a very original spin on Ireland's supposed

15 *The Round Tower at Kilbennan, surrounded by graves*

oriental connections. O'Brien's sincerely held view was that the towers were pagodas for phallic worship, erected by Zoroastrian refugees from Persia.

Petrie's success as an essayist in this competition was no cake-walk. Incredibly, the Council of the Academy was actually split on the matter, and it may have been Petrie's own reputation within that institution that tipped the judgement in his favour. O'Brien was paid £20 as runner-up, but he suspected a stitch-up: the ham-fisted way in which the Academy had set and rescinded various deadlines suggested to him that Petrie, the insider, was being given every advantage to keep improving his essay. Feeling that he had been gazumped, O'Brien brought the competition and its allegedly dodgy procedures to the public attention, and for a brief period of the 1830s the *Dublin Penny Journal* and the *Dublin University Magazine* were full of the politics of the Royal Irish Academy and of the divergent views of monuments to which the public had hitherto been largely indifferent. Thanks to the Academy's competition, and more particularly to the controversy that O'Brien had personally engendered around its result, debates about Irish historical identity began to home in on the towers, and once the debate about their origin was resolved in favour of Christianity the towers were elevated, alongside Rubensesque 'Mother Irelands', shamrocks and wolfhounds (**16**), to national icon status.

Dissatisfied that he had won only a consolation prize, O'Brien allowed the public to decide for itself the merits of his thesis. In 1834 he published it as a book. The public, it seems, quickly decided that *The Round Towers of Ireland (or the mysteries of freemasonry, of Sabaism, and of Budhism, now for the first time unveiled)* was rubbish, and O'Brien and his work disappeared from view. Either its phallic twist, intrinsically interesting for its Freudian view of the world on the eve of Victoria's reign, was too much for a genteel readership, or the public had simply grown tired of O'Brien's endless rant against the Academy!

Joep Leerssen has drawn attention to an almost Monty Pythonesque parody of the Round Towers debate and its language published in pamphlet form in 1843. It is as revealing of the seriousness with which this debate was taken in certain circles as it is hilarious as a comment on it. One 'John Flanagan' began the pamphleteering with: *A Discourse of the Round Towers of Ireland; in which the errors of the various writers on that subject are detected and confuted, and the true cause of so many differences among the learned, and the question of their use and history, is assigned and demonstrated.* In this he argued that the Round Towers did not exist at all, but that they were imagined! One 'Matthew Delany' countered with: *An answer to Mr Flanagan's extravagant assertions respecting the Round Towers of Ireland; with some original views as to their real origin and uses, and certain singular particulars on the one at Clondalkin, worthy of the attention of the curious.* In this he reports that he verified the real existence of the Clondalkin tower by testing it against all five of his senses, including taste; when he licked it he found it slightly soapy, and conjectured that it had been greased originally and that competitors scaled it in order to win a hat or bandana suspended from the top

16   *The Central Hotel, Listowel*

window by a druid! 'Flanagan' hit back with: *Delany confuted; or, an exposure of the flagitious frauds of the writer of that name in forging evidence to prove the existence of a Round Tower at Clondalkin, in the county of Dublin. With some further observations on the ancient Phoenician smelting furnace in Samcanathice, in Kilkenny!*

Petrie's thesis, meanwhile, was expanded to become a rather sumptuous volume. *The Ecclesiastical Architecture of Ireland, anterior to the Anglo-Norman Invasion, comprising an Essay on the Origin and Use of the Round Towers of Ireland*, published in 1845 (and reprinted in 1970 with an introductory essay by the late Liam de Paor), was actually intended to be part one of a two-volume work. Petrie consistently referred to supporting material in the second volume, but no such volume ever appeared.

Scholarship since Petrie in brief

Petrie's arguments about the towers were not universally accepted, even within the Royal Irish Academy. As late as 1867 Marcus Keane, an Academy member, reintroduced the worship of phalli and such things into the Round Tower debate in his *The Towers and Temples of Ancient Ireland; their Origin and History discussed from a new point of view.* But Petrie's views, for all their faults, and we will not review those faults here, constitute the base-line for serious research into early Irish ecclesiastical buildings in general and Round Towers in particular. The consensus view that was outlined in the Preface above begins to take shape between the covers of his book.

While we rightfully celebrate Petrie's book as being the first of its type, it is also, in a sense, the only one of its type. Never again was the Round Tower given so central a place in the interpretation of Irish medieval architecture. Subsequent writers on architecture, like Margaret Stokes, who listed towers and dates in her 1875-7 edition of Lord Dunraven's *Notes on Irish Architecture* and again in her own *Early Christian Art in Ireland* of 1878, and Arthur Champneys, whose excellent *Irish Ecclesiastical Architecture* appeared in 1910, recognised the importance of the towers in the story of Christian architecture in Ireland, but none emphasised them as had Petrie. Harold Leask, who wrote about the architecture of the early church in the first volume of his *Irish Churches and Monastic Buildings* trilogy in 1955, mentioned individual Round Towers in passing but virtually ignored the Round Tower as a category in its own right.

The two most comprehensive studies of Ireland's Round Towers since the mid-nineteenth century have come from non-professional scholars, but in neither case is the monument type discussed in that wider context of ecclesiastical architecture which Petrie explored. The earlier of the two books is George Lennox Barrow's *The Round Towers of Ireland*, first published in 1979 and since reprinted. Pioneering in its scope, this book was a product of careful research, reported with scrupulous honesty. Barrow's great service was to present surveys of all the existing towers. Although his actual measurements, sometimes arrived at by rather amateur means, cannot always be relied upon, and errors in detail have been pointed out over the years, his gazetteer has enduring value. His book's introductory essay, unfortunately, is fairly useless: his misunderstanding of early Ireland's history and architectural history, and his more critical denial of the historical signals emanating from annalistic sources, simply led him astray. Ironically, his erroneous account of the towers' origins and chronology led, via published reviews, other articles and books, and, most potently, word-of-mouth exchanges between scholars, to a sharpening of the consensus. The more recent book is Brian Lalor's large, readable and attractively produced *The Irish Round Tower*, published in 1999. A very useful book for anybody interested in medieval Irish buildings, this provides a wiser contextualisation of the towers than Barrow offered twenty years earlier.

Among the many other publications worth mentioning here are two journal articles and three book chapters. The two articles review earlier work: Etienne Rynne's long review of Barrow's book in the *North Munster Antiquarian Journal* for 1979 offered valuable observations hard on the heels of the original work, and Hector McDonnell's study of Margaret Stokes and her contribution, published in the *Ulster Journal of Archaeology* for 1994, restates her importance in the field and also offers some fresh perspectives. The first of the three book chapters was actually a study of Irish ecclesiastical architecture through an Anglo-Saxon lens by an English scholar, Michael Hare, published in 1986 in a volume, *The Anglo-Saxon Church*, commemorating the work of Harold Taylor, the great English buildings historian. Hare's take on the towers offered little more than Rynne in his review of Barrow, and did not explain adequately why Irish and English church architecture of the early Middle Ages differs so much, but Ann Hamlin provided a valuable appendix of historical references and their explanations to his paper. Secondly, in his book *Pilgrimage in Ireland* in 1992, Peter Harbison considered the hitherto unexplored role of the Round Tower in this most important of medieval devotional pursuits. His opinion on this matter has not received the attention it deserves, although I hope the present book helps to rectify this. Finally, in 2002 Roger Stalley published his views in a paper in a volume of collected essays, *From Ireland Coming*. This is an expansion of the views he expressed in a small booklet, *Irish Round Towers*, in 1999; his main contribution here has been with respect to the bell-ringing function of the towers.

Glasnevin and national identity again

The Glasnevin monument to 'the Liberator', Daniel O'Connell, was funded by public subscription. Petrie's original plan was to have the tower as one element of a group of monuments, the others being a Romanesque chapel and a High Cross, which would together underscore the cultural depth of historic Christian Ireland in a manner befitting its latest great hero. The tower's pairing with a church and High Cross had another motive for Petrie: having championed the view that Round Towers were ecclesiastical monuments, his scheme was intended to monumentalise the new consensus.

Petrie's dream was derailed by a shortage of funding. The Round Tower was bulked up in its scale but trimmed down in its detailing, and the two other structures were never built. This irritated him very much, as it stripped the tower of the physical indicators of its ecclesiastical origin and function.

He had an additional gripe. The famous Cork antiquarian John Windele had argued that the towers served sepulchral functions: amateur 'excavations' below the towers of Ardmore and Drumbo in 1841, Roscrea in 1842, Armoy and Kildare in 1843, Drumlane in 1844, Clones in c.1845, Kilkenny in 1846-7, and Dysert Oenghusa in 1849, had all yielded skeletal material, and he believed these to have been associated directly with the towers rather than older burials that had been disturbed by tower foundations (**17, 18**). Windele's suggestion was not entirely unreasonable: one can easily see how, for example, antiquarians familiar with prehistoric tumuli might have considered the circular plan to have had an in-built sepulchral significance, or how these same antiquaries could have been seduced by the similarities between the Irish towers and the twelfth-century western French *lanterns des morts*, themselves derived from Classical funerary architecture. Petrie had rejected, correctly we now believe, this sepulchral explanation for the Round Towers, but, to add

17 *The leaning tower of Kilmacduagh: on a misty day in the Irish midlands, the tallest Round Tower in the country rises above a huddle of churches, its lean caused by a combination of shallow foundations and old graves. Four skeletons of pre-tower date were found when its interior was dug out in 1878, confirming a pattern found at nine other sites in the 1840s*

18 *Still burying. The Round Tower at Killinaboy is one of many to stand in still-used cemeteries. Modern burials surround this truncated tower, and a modern headstone is attached to it*

insult to his injury, the committee in charge of the Glasnevin project gave their tower a burial crypt. Petrie was suspicious of the funding factor in the change of plan, and instead suspected a conspiracy: did the committee running the project have its mind changed by one of those other writers – specifically Windele – whose theories he had debunked?

There are several interconnected reasons why the Round Tower became so strong a symbol of Gaelic-Irish identity towards the end of the nineteenth century: its uniqueness to Ireland, its simple, expressive monumentality, its location on church sites, and, most critically perhaps, its interpretation as a monument-type built in defiance of Vikings, and, by extension, foreigners in general. But evidence from Connacht suggests that the understanding of the Round Tower as symbolic of Irish identity might actually pre-date the era of George Petrie and Daniel O'Connell. That Round Towers had some iconic relevance in the high Middle Ages is suggested by a small carving of a tower (based on that at Killala, several miles to the north?) on one of the supports of a very elaborate piscina in the east end of the mid-fifteenth-century Rosserk friary. More interesting from the perspective of identity is the tower which the annalists tell us was built at Annaghdown in 1238. There is a small but important group of mainly twelfth- and thirteenth-century churches at Annaghdown today, so one could easily imagine a tower here, but none survives. Since the mid-1800s there has been a suspicion that the stump of an

19 *The base of the Round Tower at Kilcoona. Is this the tower built at Annaghdown in 1238?*

20 *The expertly-constructed but now truncated Round Tower at Balla. The lower half of the upper doorway is original and of twelfth-century date, but the lower doorway was inserted in the late medieval period. Cruder ground-level doorways were inserted into other towers, at Aghagower and Aghaviller*

exceptionally well-built tower at Kilcoona, a few miles north-east of Annaghdown, is the 1238 tower (**19**); it is a reasonable suggestion since Kilcoona is a minor site, but Annaghdown was certainly important enough a place for a tower of its own. The Annaghdown reference is a rare one to the building of a tower, and it is exceptionally late; nearly sixty years separate it from the previous reference to a tower, and that earlier reference is to an older tower falling down. Given its chronological isolation, is it possible that Annaghdown was built, not to meet the same pragmatic needs for which the earlier towers were built, but as a specifically historicist statement of Gaelic identity, made in response to the Anglo-Normans successfully beginning their annexation of Connacht just three years earlier?

21 *The west tower of the parish church of Chapelizod, a late (possibly seventeenth-century) example of a circular stair turret in the former Pale*

22 *The fifteenth-century west tower at Lusk, showing the original Round Tower (partly hidden at the back on the left) imitated at the other three corners*

Round Towers might not always have connoted Gaelic-Irish identity to their spectators or owners later in the Middle Ages. Many of them were probably regarded as objects in the landscape which deserved to be preserved only because they could be used in some practical way: they remained useful as bell-houses for later medieval churches, and ground-level doorways were sometimes inserted to facilitate that use (**20**). In the fifteenth-century Pale, the land around Dublin in which there remained some loyalty to the English crown long after it had evaporated elsewhere, it was not unusual for cylindrical stair turrets to be built as parts of tower-houses or, more rarely, church towers (**21**); the stairs here were just like the spiral stairs inside contemporary buildings, but by projecting them outwards in semi-engaged turrets more interior space was made available. At Lusk (**22**) and Duleek (**colour plate 3**), two sites in the English Pale, actual Round Towers of pre-Norman date were simply converted into church towers. One could suggest that these adaptations by late medieval English families were made with some recognition of the towers' cultural origins, but that may be to falsely credit them – and the wider world of the fifteenth and sixteenth centuries – with actually caring about such matters.

That 'land of saints and scholars' catchphrase with which this chapter began exists today mainly in tourism-speak; one need only listen to a guided tour at one of Ireland's great medieval monasteries to feel how alive it is, in some shape or form, in the heritage industry. Modern scholarship is far too sensitive to the complexities of the ancient past to fall for any platitude which reduces the population to two such noble categories; there was too much violence, too much farming, too much ordinariness in early Ireland for that. And modern Ireland certainly possesses no such rose-tinted view of itself either: modern Irish people, harbouring no illusions that the country has fewer social ills than any other, sometimes wheel out the expression about saints and scholars but do so sarcastically. The heritage artefacts which nourished burgeoning Irish identity in the nineteenth and twentieth centuries are no longer such potent bearers of cultural nationalism but are recognised internationally as items of world heritage value. But ideas of 'Irishness' are still sometimes manifest around them. One might identify, for example, traces of older political disputes in the continued disagreement between Irish and British scholars on the place of manufacture of the Book of Durrow. And one can certainly detect a particular ideology at work in the recent erection of a Round Tower – using stone from, of all things, an old famine workhouse – as the centrepiece of the Irish war memorial in Messines in Belgium.

2
The enduring template
Round Tower architecture
and its chronology

The 'classic' Irish Round Tower is a *free-standing* structure, obviously cylindrical, which is usually to be found close to and on the north-west or south-west side of a church. There are sixty-four of these towers, of which fifteen survive only at foundation level (**23**) or at least do not rise to doorway height (**24**). One tower – that on Ram's Island in Lough Neagh – survives to at least half its original height but its openings have been filled in so that it is virtually featureless. The majority of towers, then, survive to an appreciable height (**25**, **26**), with twenty-one of these – about 30 per cent of the overall total – being fairly complete (**27**). Adding the evidence of destroyed towers in the annalistic and antiquarian records to this figure allows us to estimate that pre-Norman Ireland had as many as ninety free-standing Round Towers.

Round Towers were sometimes also attached to churches, either as integral features of those churches as originally built, or, a little more rarely, as additions which were accommodated by making some structural alterations to the churches. At four northern sites – Dungiven, Killeevy, Tamlaght and Trummery – the now-demolished towers rose off rectangular lower storeys which still remain. Something similar still stands far away at Ferns in south-east Ireland, and there was another, clearly a secondary feature, at Trinity Church at Glendalough. St Kevin's at Glendalough (**28**) and St Michael le Pole in Dublin had relatively small towers rising out of the west ends of their church roofs, while a tower rose over the chancel of the small church at Kilmacnessan. Temple Finghin at Clonmacnoise, finally, has its tower at the junction of the nave and chancel (**29**).

Scholars have been uncertain about how to treat these 'attached' towers. Lennox Barrow, for example, excluded them from his list of Round Towers, whereas Brian Lalor included them in his. Now, the basic architectural and aesthetic templates that were used for free-standing towers were occasionally used for these 'attached' towers, so that towers of both categories actually

23 *The fragmentary Round Tower at Ardrahan*

24 *Conservation beyond the call of duty? The patched-up Round Tower at Aghadoe*

looked alike, but the free-standing towers were conceptually different in that they constituted a separate ritual focus on their church sites so all activities associated with them occurred in full view (**30** and **colour plate 6**). The 'attached' towers belong in a lineage that leads via buildings like the so-called Belfry church on Inchcleraun (**31**) to towers like those that we have already encountered in the Pale; to that extent, therefore, I would tend to side with Barrow's view of them as something quite different.

The distribution of all these towers, free-standing and attached, is remarkable for its near-blanket coverage of Ireland. It even extends to some of the offshore islands (**32**), undermining what might be the popular understanding of remote western Irish monasteries as places resistant to change. The main concentration of towers is actually spread in a great U-shape, from central Connacht to Thomond (the Shannon estuary area), across the south midlands, and back up through east Leinster as far as south Ulster. There are gaps – central and western Ulster, the north midlands and south Munster had comparatively few towers – but on the whole the Round Tower was an island-wide phenomenon. Whether it was island-wide at the very start is debatable. The fact that virtually all the documented towers are in the northern half of Ireland, including the earliest known example at Slane, does seem to reflect a pattern of record-keeping and nothing more: lightning bolts and big winds were not, after all, confined to the north. Also, the second earliest reference to a tower is to one at Tuamgraney, which is in the south of Ireland. However, the northern weighting of the references, and also perhaps the frequency of sites with Patrician associations – associated with St Patrick, in other words – on the list of towers, inclines one to believe that in this area there was a special regard for, or special awareness of, towers, indicating perhaps that the earliest towers were in this half of Ireland. Indeed, if the Round Tower made its debut appearance as a fully formed monument type in any one single place in Ireland, Armagh, the primatial see, would surely be most people's choice.

Design templates

The elevation drawings in **25** and **26** give a good impression of the towers' visual consistency, but there is some variation in their details (the numbers, shapes and arrangements of the openings), and that variation is perhaps best represented by unfolding the towers as is done in the drawings accompanying this section of the book. These drawings are intended more as graphics than as actual metrically correct representations: the batters, or tapers, for example, which are so striking a feature of many towers, especially the two twelfth-century towers of Dysert Oenghusa and Ardmore (**colour plates 7** and **8**), are flattened out here.

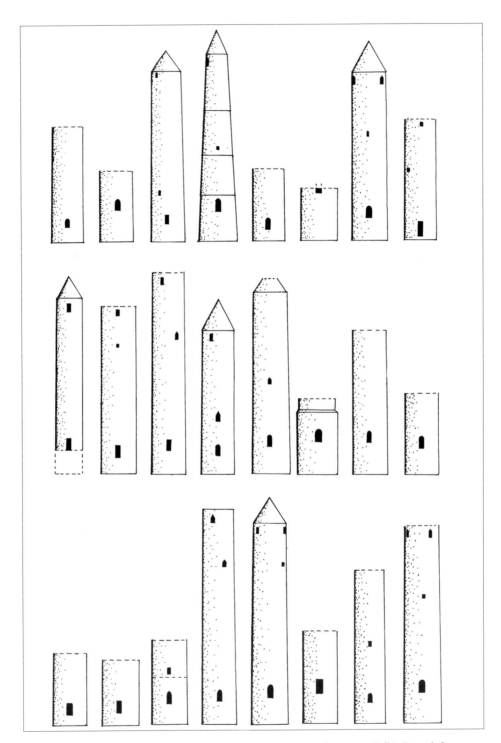

25 *Entrance elevations of Round Towers with surviving doorways (Aghagower to Kells).* From left to right, top row: *Aghagower, Aghaviller, Antrim, Ardmore, Armoy, Balla, Cashel, Castledermot.* Middle row: *Clondalkin, Clones, Cloyne, Devenish, Donaghmore, Dysert O'Dea, Dysert Oenghusa, Dromiskin.* Bottom row: *Drumbo, Drumcliff (Sligo), Drumlane, Fertagh, Glendalough, Inishkeen, Inis Cealtra, Kells*

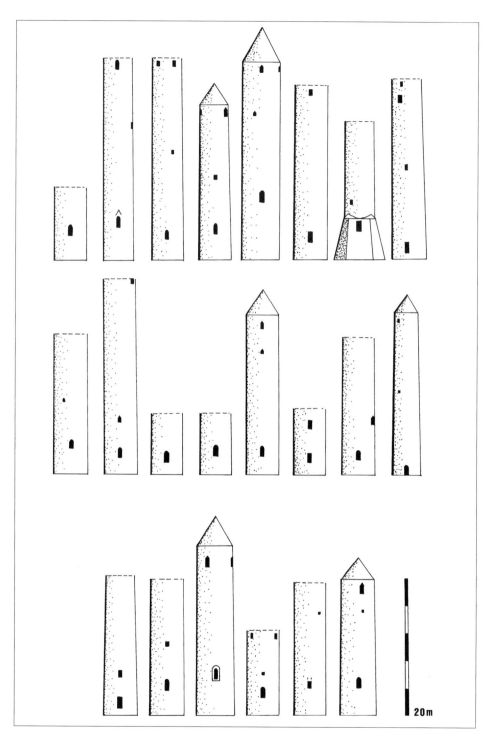

26 *Entrance elevations of Round Towers with surviving doorways (Kilbennan to Turlough).* From left to right, top row: *Kilbennan, Kildare, Kilkenny, Killala, Kilmacduagh, Kilree, Kinneigh, Lusk.* Middle row: *Meelick, Monasterboice, Old Kilcullen, Oughterard, Rattoo, Roscam, Roscrea, Scattery Island.* Bottom row: *Swords, Taghadoe, Timahoe, Tory, Tullaherin, Turlough*

27 *A virtually complete Round Tower at Kilkenny, rising over the gable of the south transept of the adjoining cathedral. Like so many other examples, it has lost its cap, and there is now a medieval parapet in its place*

28 *St Kevin's church, Glendalough, from the east, showing the arch of the now-destroyed chancel and the small tower over the nave; the church has a complex restoration history*

29 Above *A Round Tower is physically part of Temple Finghin at Clonmacnoise; seemingly an original part of the church, it probably dates to the third quarter of the twelfth century. In the background, the River Shannon is in full flood*

30 Left *Fertagh, one of the most elegant of Round Towers*

31 Opposite above *The Belfry church on Inchcleraun may date to c.1200; the square western tower which gives it its name is an early addition.*

32 Opposite below *Killeany Round Tower, on land sloping down to the Atlantic.*

The drawings are arranged here according to a simple classification of tower doorways, since the doorways provide the most useful clues to tower chronology. Two important consistencies to be noted at the outset are the general clockwise (or right-to-left, then back to right-to-left again, in the accompanying drawings) ascent of the windows in the tower drums and the frequency with which four windows mark the uppermost (or bell-) storeys. These consistencies are, arguably, more important than the variations in detail.

The towers at the three Dublin sites of Clondalkin, Lusk and Swords, and at Clones, Antrim, Kinneigh, Roscam and Castledermot, have lintelled openings throughout, giving these buildings a rather plain character (**33**, **34** and **colour plate 9** *top*). Directly above the lintel of the doorway of the tower at Antrim is a stone bearing a carving of a small ringed cross standing on a pedestal, so this gave an otherwise plain tower a little visual relief. Both Kinneigh and Roscam of this group are incomplete, so it is conceivable that other window designs were used higher up. Kinneigh is an unusual tower, rising as it does off a six-sided base. These sites are quite widely distributed, with all four sides of the island (Antrim, Galway, Cork and Dublin) represented.

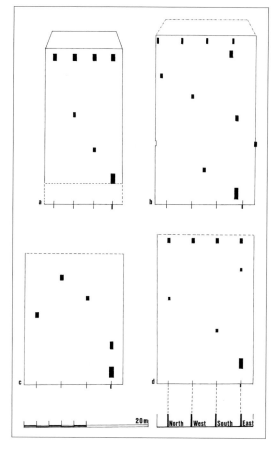

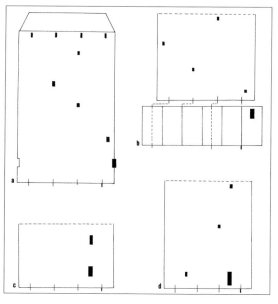

33 Left *Folded-out schematic drawings of Round Towers with lintelled doorways and lintelled (extant) windows: (a) Clondalkin; (b) Lusk; (c) Swords; (d) Clones*

34 Above *Folded-out schematic drawings of Round Towers with lintelled doorways and lintelled (extant) windows: (a) Antrim; (b) Kinneigh; (c) Roscam; (d) Castledermot. Same scale as figure 33*

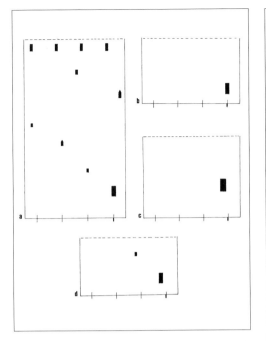

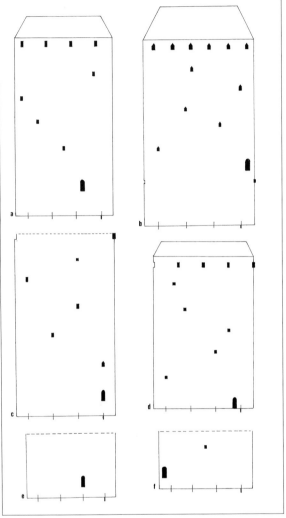

35 Above *Folded-out schematic drawings of Round Towers with lintelled doorways:*
(a) Cloyne; (b) Drumbo; (c) Inishkeen;
(d) Drumcliff (Sligo). Same scale as figure 33

36 Right *Folded-out schematic drawings of Round Towers with monolithic or semi-corbelled doorways: (a) Glendalough; (b) Kilmacduagh;*
(c) Monasterboice; (d) Scattery Island;
(e) Armoy; (f) Old Kilcullen. Same scale as figure 33

Lintelled doorways are also a feature of the towers of Cloyne, Drumbo, Inishkeen, and Drumcliff in Sligo (**35**). Cloyne is a fairly complete tower which also has angle-headed openings. The other three towers are fragmentary so it is possible that they too displayed some variety in the design of their openings.

Doorways with arched tops either cut out of single stones (these are called monolithic arches) or using some form of corbelling (which means that the arch is built up with horizontal layers) link the towers of Glendalough, Kilmacduagh, Monasterboice, Scattery Island, Armoy and Old Kilcullen (**36** and **colour plate 9** *bottom*).

Round-arched doorways with voussoirs (the wedge-shaped stones that make up an arch) but without any other embellishment of their exteriors are the most common of all in Round Towers. The towers which possess them are at

Inis Cealtra, Clonmacnoise, Kilbennan, Aghagower, Meelick, Oughterard, Dysert O'Dea (**37**), Killala, Kilkenny, Turlough and Tory (**38**).

Architraves, or slightly raised, flat-surfaced surrounds, are found on round arches at Drumlane, Cashel, Aghaviller, Taghadoe (**39**), Kilree (where the arch is actually monolithic), Rattoo, Roscrea, Kells and Donaghmore (**40**). The towers at Tullaherin and Fertagh probably had round-arched doorways originally (**41**).

Among these towers Taghadoe, Kells and Donaghmore form a small group in their own right by virtue of the sculptural treatment of their doorways. Above the doorway at Taghadoe is a defaced sculpture, presumably a head (**colour plate 10** *top*). A similar, and similarly defaced, feature flanks one side of the doorway at Kells, and there may have been a second such feature on the other side of the doorway (**colour plate 10** *bottom left*). The Kells doorway is clearly an insert into an older tower, identifiable perhaps with the tower

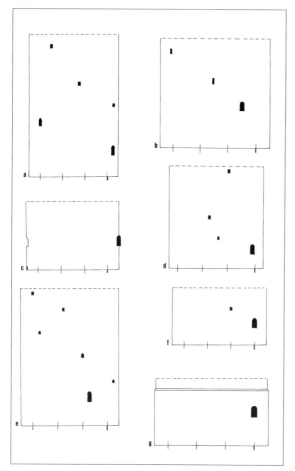

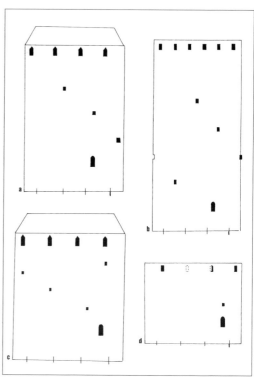

38   Right *Folded-out schematic drawings of Round Towers with round-arched doorways without architraves: (a) Killala; (b) Kilkenny; (c) Turlough; (d) Tory. Same scale as figure 33*

37   Left *Folded-out schematic drawings of Round Towers with round-arched doorways without architraves: (a) Inis Cealtra; (b) Clonmacnoise; (c) Kilbennan; (d) Aghagower; (e) Meelick; (f) Oughterard; (g) Dysert O'Dea. Same scale as figure 33*

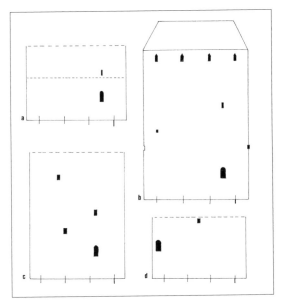

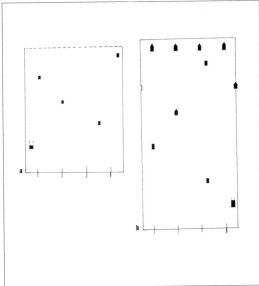

39 Above *Folded-out schematic drawings of Round Towers with round-arched doorways with architraves: (a) Drumlane; (b) Cashel; (c) Aghaviller; (d) Taghadoe. Same scale as figure 33*

40 Right *Folded-out schematic drawings of Round Towers with round-arched doorways with architraves: (a) Kilree; (b) Rattoo; (c) Roscrea, (d) Kells, (e) Donaghmore. Same scale as figure 33*

41 Above right *Folded-out schematic drawings of Round Towers which probably had round-arched doorways: (a) Tullaherin; (b) Fertagh. Same scale as figure 33*

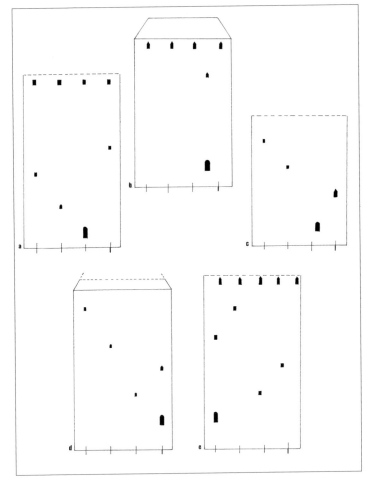

mentioned by the annalists in 1076. The doorway of Donaghmore, which might not be original to its tower, has two defaced heads on either side, and a curious carving of Christ above the arch (**colour plate 10** *bottom right*). Donaghmore tower is very odd indeed: it is the only tower without upper storey windows (**colour plate 11**). The doorway of the tower at Dromiskin, which belongs in that final group of towers enumerated in the next paragraph, also has a pair of flanking heads pushed out to the sides of the doorway jambs (**colour plate 12**).

Finally, there are the towers with decorative devices characteristic of Gaelic-Irish Romanesque architecture of the 1100s. We will discuss these in some detail below, so we can just list them here. They are Kildare, Timahoe, Ardmore, Devenish (**42**), Dysert Oenghusa, Balla and Dromiskin (**43**). One of these, Devenish, has a doorway which would suggest it is better included in the same category as, say, Rattoo, but it is featured in this group for reasons which we will see.

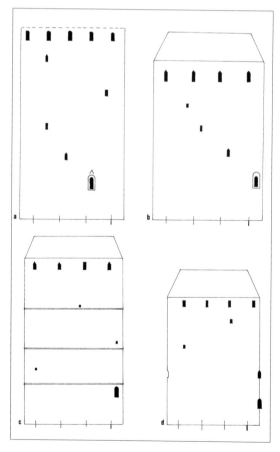

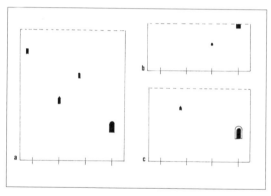

42 Left *Folded-out schematic drawings of Round Towers with twelfth-century Romanesque features: (a) Kildare; (b) Timahoe; (c) Ardmore; (d) Devenish. Same scale as figure 33*

43 Above *Folded-out schematic drawings of Round Towers with twelfth-century Romanesque features: (a) Dysert Oenghusa; (b) Balla; (c) Dromiskin. Same scale as figure 33*

Spatial and metrical templates

Round Towers were built in consistent or recurring spatial relationships with churches. They almost always stood several tens of metres to the west of a principal church. More specifically, they were placed to that church's north-west (**44**) or south-west (**45**). There are only rare exceptions. At Scattery, for example, the tower stands almost due west of the cathedral (**46**), while at Castledermot the tower stands to the north of the present church (itself a replacement of a medieval church) and to the east of a line connecting that site's two extant High Crosses. If their positions are unusual, so too are their designs: both the Scattery and Castledermot towers have ground-floor doorways rather than the elevated doorways that one finds elsewhere. These factors have been adduced as evidence that these are early (i.e. tenth-century) towers; interestingly, Margaret Stokes recorded a tradition ascribing the erection of Castledermot to an abbot who died in 919. It has even been suggested that Scattery, a particularly idiosyncratic tower, was the prototype for the entire Irish Round Tower series. One could, of course, argue the opposite, which is that the Scattery and Castledermot towers were knowing deviations from an established norm and that they are, therefore, quite late. Apropos of Scattery's primacy, it is a little unlikely that the Round Towers originated in southern Ireland, and it is highly improbable that the place of origin was in a small river-island monastery in southern Ireland of which the founder saint enjoyed a local rather than regional or national devotion.

44 *The Round Tower and church at Kilree, viewed from the south. The tower stands slightly to the north-west of the church; the buttresses against the church wall are later features*

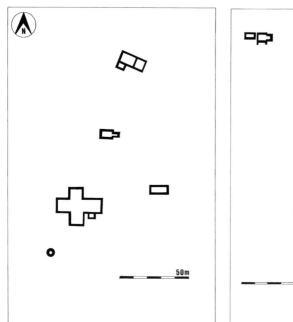 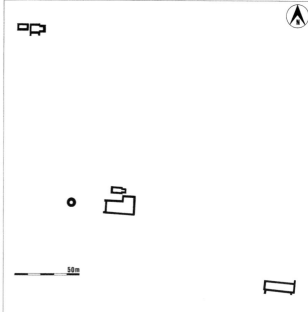

45 Left *Map of Kilmacduagh showing the Round Tower standing to the south-west of the cathedral, an eleventh-century and later church. The northernmost building in this map is known as the glebe house, a later thirteenth-century hall, and to the south of it is the church of St John the Baptist, possibly eleventh century in date. To the south-east is St Mary's church (also known as Templemurray), c.1200 and later. Another church in the group, the very fine O'Heyne's church dating from c.1200, is further north*

46 Right *Map of Scattery Island showing the Round Tower west of the cathedral (eleventh to fourteenth century), with a small, probably twelfth-century, nave-and-chancel church immediately to its north, a conjoined tomb-chapel and church (Templesenan) of uncertain date to the north-west, and the late medieval Templenamarve (the church of the dead) to the south-east. Another church to the south-west is not shown here*

Apparently the spatial relationships between towers and churches, and High Crosses where they are found, were carefully established or manufactured on the ground. More detailed survey work at sites with towers is needed, but scrutiny of a number of sites reveals a pattern, as at Monasterboice (**47** and **colour plate 13**) and Clonmacnoise (**48**), for example. Spatiality sometimes also involved proportional schemes: at Glendalough the length of the nave of the nearby great church – designated a cathedral in the early twelfth century – is three times the diameter of the tower, suggesting that the church and tower are contemporary, while at Inis Cealtra the church nave is twice the tower's diameter, again suggesting contemporaneity. Such relationships seem to be consistent with the evidence of a tantalising commentary on an early law, now known only in a later medieval recension (Trinity College Dublin manuscript H 3 17), giving a series of interdependent prices for the building of stone churches, timber churches and bell-houses, and also indicating that the basal

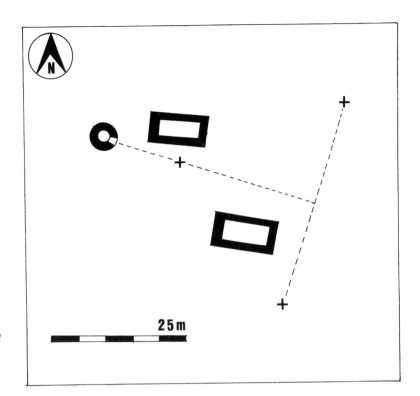

47 *Plan of Monasterboice showing how the High Crosses and Round Tower are aligned*

25 m

Cathedral
+ High Cross

Round Tower

50 m

48 *Plan of Clonmacnoise showing the alignments of the three High Crosses and Round Tower and their spatial relationship to the Great Church*

measurement (the diameter?) and height of a tower could be evaluated for pricing purposes against the measurements of its associated stone church.

Did these towers also have a metrical consistency in and of themselves? Before answering this, some words of caution. Calculating units of measurement and working out proportional systems for any ancient building or monument is a hazardous task. Measurement units were not consistent across ancient and medieval time and space, and even that standard unit of measure in the Middle Ages – the foot – was not standardised in its length: the Roman foot or *pes monetalis*, for example, measured about 29.3cm in modern length, the Roman *pes drusianus* was nearly 33.3cm long, the so-called 'Northern' foot' was about 33.5cm long, and the medieval English foot was equivalent to the modern imperial foot of 30.5cm. So, divining ancient or medieval units of measure is difficult for the modern scholar. Special caution is also required with respect to reconstructing systems of proportion: with a ruler and compass and a ground plan it is usually possible to establish some complex set of mathematical and geometrical relationships for any site, but it is generally the case that the more complex the relationship suggested by the ruler and compass the more likely it is to be an invention of the analyst rather than a rediscovery. When detected, simple proportional schemes like 1:1, 1:1.5, 1:2 and so on, can generally be trusted as real, in part because there are obvious practical ways of laying them out, and in part because fairly simple mathematics are required for sizes to be calculated at these ratios. The same is true of particular proportions, such as $1:\sqrt{2}$ (or 1:1.4142) and $1:\Phi$ (or $1:\frac{1}{2}(\sqrt{5}+1)$, approximately 1:1.618, known as the Golden Section), which were used in Classical architecture and were known about in the Middle Ages precisely because theses of Classical writers on architecture were preserved.

Glendalough's Round Tower (**49**) can be used as a case-study to prize open the issue of Round Tower metrology. It has the most exact measurements of all the towers: it has a ground-level circumference of 50ft (±6 inches to allow for variations in the surface of the stone, and therefore within a 1 per cent tolerance), a diameter of almost 16ft (which is 6 inches short of the size of a standard medieval perch), and a height of 100ft (±6 inches again) to the top of its rebuilt (but accurately so) conical roof. Its circumference is 1½ft below the average for all the extant towers, and, accordingly, its diameter is also below average. In fact, its diameter falls more than a metre short of the largest diameter measurement of all, which is that of Oran Round Tower (**50, 51**).

The Glendalough circumference-to-height ratio of 1:2 may have been a feature of other towers as well: of those which survive to near their full original height, the towers at Cloyne, Donaghmore, Fertagh, Kells, Kildare, Kilkenny, Kilmacduagh, Kilree, Lusk and Monasterboice probably fitted the pattern. Antrim might also be included here; its top is a little lower in height than the ratio requires, but it has been repaired. The towers at Ardmore, Cashel and Rattoo are a little shorter than twice their circumferences, while the tower at

49 *The Round Tower at Glendalough; the cap was rebuilt in 1876*

50 Above *The base of a once-substantial Round Tower at Oran with its toupée of ivy*

51 Below *Close-up of the masonry at Oran.*

Clondalkin is a little taller. The mid-twelfth-century tower at Timahoe is 2ft taller than the height that would correspond to a ratio of 1:Φ, but the comparable tower at Devenish, of the late twelfth century, is within 6 inches of this ratio. It must be pointed out that some towers were simply short. Tory Island's tower had all the ingredients of a Glendalough-type tower but it did not stand much higher than it does today (**52**). There is antiquarian evidence that the tower at Old Kilcullen was of equally low height. The tower at Ardpatrick (**53**) stood on so exposed a hill-top site that it cannot have risen particularly high; its considerable ruination may, of course, be a result of its having been built too high. At least one tower – that at Dromiskin (**54**) – was lowered in the Middle Ages and given a new cap imitative of its original.

Glendalough is the most perfectly proportioned of all the towers which stand to or near full height. Its 50ft circumference is equalled to within 6 inches at other, now truncated, towers (Aghaviller, Clones, Drumcliff (Sligo), Inishkeen, Kilbennan, Killeany, Maghera, Roscrea and Tullaherin). On the

52 *The low-height Round Tower on Tory Island*

53 *The fragmentary Round Tower at Ardpatrick*

basis of Glendalough and towers of similar height we can suggest that a circum-ference-to-height ratio of 1:2 was optimal. It is not possible to say how seriously such an optimal ratio was taken, or if it was widely observed. Nor do we know if the earliest towers respected this ratio or if the towers gravitated towards this ratio over time. One imagines that the earlier towers adhered more strictly to design rules than the later ones. It certainly does not help our work in this area that so few towers have their upper portions intact.

The architectural dating of Round Towers

We have many reasons to be grateful to the annalists who mentioned Round Towers in their clipped records of the early Middle Ages, not least because their chronicles reveal the durability of the Round Tower as both idea and physical structure over a period of some three hundred years. It is very doubtful if archaeologists would suspect that the corpus of sixty or so extant towers was created over so long a period, even allowing for the relatively slow rate of archi-tectural development in pre-Norman Ireland. The likelihood is that we would condense the dating into a span of no more than a century and a half, from the early eleventh to the later twelfth centuries. Assuming the earliest towers to have been comparable in form and function with the extant towers, many of which

54 *Dromiskin Round Tower. This is a twelfth-century tower. Its present appearance – like a short, stumpy pencil standing on end – is the product of a reroofing of what was probably a ruin. The clue is a small, angle-headed window just underneath the bell-storey*

clearly date to the eleventh and twelfth centuries as we will see here, one must be struck by the continuity of design over the length of more than a dozen lifetimes. Yes, doorway and window designs differed from tower to tower and they certainly changed over time, but the basic template remained consistent.

The survival rate of documented towers after 1076 is quite good, but none of the towers mentioned before that survives, and that is hugely unfortunate for the purposes of understanding the architectural development of the entire group. With so few annalistic records of tower construction, we are heavily dependent on archaeological strategies for establishing chronology.

By looking carefully at the fabric we can sometimes see *relative* chronology, particularly in the top parts of towers where later generations repaired or replaced what acts of nature or violence removed (**colour plate 14**). But our dating of the towers to actual or *absolute* periods of time is, for the most part, stylistic.

Before looking at how stylistic dating works, we should acknowledge there is a scientific method for dating the towers: tiny quantities of charcoal found in mortar can be dated by radiocarbon analysis. A number of early medieval buildings in Ireland have been dated in this way, and the dates obtained often tally with the dates suggested by more conventional architectural-historical methods. The tower at Rattoo (**55**), for example, has been radiocarbon-dated to the later eleventh century, which tallies with the date which the building's details would suggest. Just as it revolutionised prehistoric archaeology decades ago, radiocarbon dating of mortar may revolutionise our understanding of the architectural chronology of the early church, at least with respect to mortared buildings. But we must be careful not to allow it automatically be the sole arbiter of date: the best approach to medieval dates that are obtained by scientific method is to judge their merits against dates that might be suggested by other, seemingly less 'objective', means. There may sometimes be cultural or stylistic reasons for rejecting a scientifically obtained date.

Stylistic dating is problematic. First, we have few fixed points against which to judge stylistic developments: there are very few historical references to any of the extant towers, and we have no record that any one of our surviving towers was extant in the tenth century. We can import some stylistic arguments from the world of church architecture to help us date some towers to the twelfth century, and indeed to within periods of three decades or so within that century, but we know too little about the chronology of church architecture in the 900s and in most of the 1000s to identify those towers that belong to that period. Secondly, stylistic dating is often based on Darwinian assumptions about stylistic progression or improvement, and yet the 'style' of a building may simply reflect the monetary or material resources available at the time of construction. Also, artists or builders, and their patrons, might sometimes have opted for archaisms in their work. So, the fact that some detail looks 'old' does not mean that it is old; one need only look at *modern* so-called

55 *Rattoo Round Tower, viewed through a fifteenth-century window*

Georgian windows (usually made of PVC) to know this. Nonetheless, that principle of stylistic progression through time guides the chronology of the Round Towers in most of the literature, with relatively simple towers of unsophisticated construction, like Clones (**56**), being regarded as early in the sequence. It is an opinion encouraged by the fact that well-built towers with dressed openings, as at Ardmore in particular (**57**), are certainly relatively late in date.

Using church architecture as our guide, two general, sequential groups of Round Towers can be identified. The earlier is of *c.*1050-*c.*1130 date, and it corresponds roughly to the towers in **36-40**, above. The 1130 date which brackets this period is based on the fact that architectural style in Ireland underwent a change about that time, spurred on by the appearance in southern Ireland of a particular repertoire of decorative forms or motifs from the

56 Left *The (tenth-century?) Round Tower at Clones*

57 Opposite *The (twelfth-century) Round Tower at Ardmore*

Romanesque tradition of Norman England. The *c.*1050 date is more notional, but I will defend it in a moment. The later of the two groups is of general post-1130 date, and it corresponds to the towers in **42** and **43**. All of the towers in these two groups can probably be described as Romanesque, if one wishes to use that term, while the post-1130 towers are of the classic Irish (or Hiberno-) Romanesque tradition which uses roll-mouldings and chevrons and so on.

Eleventh and early twelfth-century towers

Twenty-one towers are identified within this group on the basis of having round-arched doorways devoid of that type of decoration that one finds after about 1130. Doorway type or style is a rather uncertain means of assessing chronology, but I think one could be fairly confident that most if not all of these towers were built in the century or so before 1130.

The arches of these doorways fall into two basic categories. In the first, the voussoirs are neatly cut both underside (the soffit) and topside (the extrados), as at Clonmacnoise (**58**), a Round Tower that was completed, according to the annalists, in 1124. A similar arch-ring is found in St Kevin's church at

58 *The doorway of Clonmacnoise Round Tower, made about 1120*

59 *The lintelled doorway with a round relieving arch and tympanum of St Kevin's church, Glendalough; the lintel is the wrong way around, indicating that there has been some rebuilding work here*

Glendalough, probably built about 1100 (**59**). The other, more numerous, category has arches which are neatly cut just on their undersides, as for example at Roscrea (**60**) and Meelick (**61**). Although a little cruder, these should not be regarded as earlier in date than the type found at Clonmacnoise: builders did not always bother to dress the topsides of arch stones, even in the mid-twelfth century (**62**).

Why do we date these arched doorways – and the towers in which they feature – to this particular period? It is partly on negative grounds: we expect post-1130 doorways to be more elaborate. It is also partly on comparative grounds. The true arch, by which is meant an arch made with voussoirs, seems only to appear in church architecture in the later eleventh and early twelfth centuries. It was used specifically for the chancel arches of a small number of churches, and yet the churches in question (**63**) continued to possess the older, lintelled, form of doorway. Indeed, the type of round-arched doorway which we find in the Round Towers was used very rarely in churches, so it is tempting to suggest that the first true arches in Ireland were those in the towers. If true arches were in use in Round Tower doorways over a long period of time – before, say, 1050 – we might expect to find them being replicated on church doorways; in fact, the opposite happens: rather than churches borrow from Round Towers, the towers seem to borrow from the churches (**64, 65**).

60 Above *The doorway of Roscrea Round Tower*

61 Left *The round-arched doorway of Meelick Round Tower showing how the voussoirs continue through the thickness of the wall*

63 Opposite below: *A round chancel arch with plain imposts, c.1100, associated with a lintelled doorway at Palmerstown. It is possible that the arch and the chancel beyond it were added to a smaller, simpler church, but the lintelled west door was still retained*

62   Above *An interior view of the paired east windows of mid-twelfth-century date in Aghowle church. On the exterior these windows have chevron decoration of the classic, post-1130, Gaelic-Irish Romanesque tradition*

64 *Drumlane Round Tower. Its doorway has an architrave of the type that one finds on lintelled church doorways (see **65**)*

65 *The architraved west doorway of Tuamgraney church, built in the mid-900s*

66 *The bell-storey of the Round Tower at Cashel*

One final point is that most of these towers have angle-headed windows (**66**) either in their drums, or in their bell-storeys, or in both. This pattern continues into the twelfth century in the towers discussed below. One of the angle-headed bell-storey windows at Rattoo has a sheela-na-gig carved on it, while an angle-headed window from a now-destroyed tower at Tomregan is decorated with a remarkable male exhibitionist figure (**67**). After the simple lintel top, the angle-head was the most popular method for finishing off a window in Round Tower architecture; it was not used for doorways. Round-arched windows, though, are quite rare in towers, and where they are found they are monolithic; in other words, the arch is cut out of a stone rather than made by using voussoirs.

Towers after 1130

The later towers, of which there are seven widely distributed examples, are the most securely dated of all the towers. The 1130 date given here is derived from the 1127-1130 date-range of Cormac's Chapel at Cashel, the small but beau-tifully-crafted Romanesque church on the Rock of Cashel (**68**). The type of embellished Romanesque architecture which one finds in it matches what we find on these seven towers. Cormac's Chapel was probably not the earliest

67 *The ex situ window head from Tomregan Round Tower, photographed in the grounds of Ballyconnell church near the original site*

68   *Cormac's Chapel as depicted in Petrie's* Ecclesiastical Architecture of Ireland

church to have this type of architecture in Ireland, but it was one of the very first, and it is the earliest to survive intact.

The finest of the later towers is, of course, that at Ardmore, one of Ireland's best known medieval buildings. Its exact date is not known. Its very distinctive string-coursing (**colour plate 8** *top*) can actually be paralleled on the towers of Cormac's Chapel. Its doorway (**colour plate 8** *bottom*) is of a rare type; there was a similar doorway in an Augustinian priory church at Corbally but very little remains of it. The roll-moulding which enframes the doorway is a classic detail of the sculpturally embellished Romanesque work that one finds in Ireland in the second and third quarters of the twelfth century. Corbels projecting inwards from the inside of the tower drum are decorated with motifs – human and animal heads, and abstract forms – of similar vintage.

There are clues in the topography of the site to support a mid-twelfth-century date for the Ardmore tower. Its doorway faces two buildings. One is the 'tomb-chapel' called St Declan's 'House', a pre-Romanesque building possibly of tenth-century date if not earlier (**69**). The other is the pre-Romanesque (tenth-century?) church which was converted into the chancel of Ardmore Cathedral in the twelfth century. This orientation suggests the tower pre-dates the cathedral in its developed, late twelfth-century, state, and on that basis it is possible to suggest an 1130-70 date range. It may have been built to support Ardmore's claim to episcopal status in 1152.

Moving on alphabetically, we head north to Balla (see **19**). This is an exceptionally well-built tower, with regularly coursed, semi-ashlar blocks which are dressed to the curvature of the wall. It survives to a little above the top of its upper doorway. The top has been trimmed off to a consistent horizontal level. The stone courses are all narrow until just above the sill level of the upper doorway, at which point the individual stones become noticeably larger. That upper doorway (**70**) is lintelled. Its lower jamb stones have traces of Romanesque roll mouldings which are suggestive of a twelfth-century date, and the moulding on the basal off-set of the tower would be consistent with

69 *St Declan's 'House' at Ardmore, traditionally the burial place of St Declan, Ardmore's founder saint. The slight remains of* antae, *short projections of the side walls past the end walls, can be seen at both gable ends. These features, which would originally have risen to roof level, are frequently found on early medieval and Romanesque churches in Ireland*

70   *The doorway of Balla Round Tower*

this. The plain character of the remainder of the doorway's jamb stones, and indeed of the lintel, suggests that they represent a later replacement of post-1130 Romanesque work. Given that this change in the nature of the doorway is at the same level as the change in the masonry of the drum, it is very likely that this upper part of the tower was built in the late Middle Ages, reusing stone which had originally came from higher up the tower; the lintel and the unmoulded sections of the jambs may even have come from an upper-floor window. The lower, pointed-arched doorway into the tower is late medieval, and it may have been inserted about the time that the top of the tower was reconstructed.

Devenish is a particularly beautiful tower (**71**). The cornice – the ridge of masonry between the top of the drum and the bottom of the cap – is decorated with carved scrolls and pellets of typical post-1130 Romanesque type, and there are four human heads, also of a familiar Romanesque type, positioned directly above the bell-storey windows (**72**). The date of the tower is uncertain but it may belong to the period after 1176, as we will see below (see p.110). Curiously, the tower's doorway is not embellished with comparable details (**73**). It is worth noting, if only as a cautionary tale, that we would not regard Devenish as a post-1130 tower if fate had deprived us of its cornice and cap.

71   *The Round Tower at Devenish*

North

East

South

West

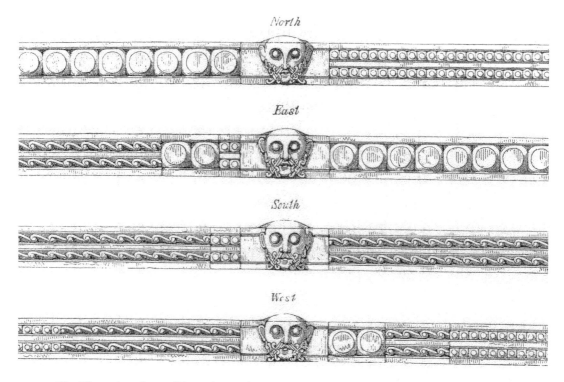

72 *The cornice sculpture of Devenish Round Tower as depicted in Petrie's* Ecclesiastical Architecture of Ireland

Also in the northern half of Ireland is the little-discussed tower at Dromiskin. Here is a very interesting building indeed. Its doorway (**74**) belongs within the English Romanesque tradition of the later eleventh and twelfth centuries: it is round-arched and recessed, with narrow columns (now missing) tucked into the returns (the recesses) and finished off with (now-worn) capitals. There is a very slight ledge on each side of the inner doorway immediately underneath the round arch, and, while this may be a result of some reconstruction work, it is conceivable that there was a tympanum or D-shaped stone here, such as one finds at, say, Jarrow (**75**), to choose a random parallel from England.

How old is the Dromiskin doorway? This is a difficult question to answer. There are no exactly comparable doorways in Ireland, even in churches. But there are some church doorways with small, detached, columns tucked into the return-angles of recessed jambs in Munster, where they date from the first half of the twelfth century. The earliest example (in a small church at Killaloe) may date from the late eleventh century, but the very small number of examples is generally of 1120-1150 date. Were we to find a Dromiskin-type doorway in Kerry or Tipperary we would have no hesitation dating it to the period before 1150, nor would we blink if we found some historical reason to date it to, say, 1120. This could, then, be an early twelfth-century work.

73 Left *The doorway of the Round Tower at Devenish, with its modern steps and incongruous painted wrought-iron trimmings*

74 Below *The doorway of Dromiskin Round Tower*

75 *A Romanesque doorway (repaired) at Jarrow; the tympanum here is formed of three stones*

Our next tower is in Munster, at Dysert Oenghusa (**colour plate 7**). This has a rather unusual doorway. It has an architrave, as per the older round-arched doorways of Round Towers which we discussed above, but cut into it is a hollow channel filled with small beads or pellets (**76**), a fairly typical device of post-1130 date. Similar decoration can be found elsewhere in the Limerick-Clare-Tipperary region, albeit in imprecisely dated churches (Temple Cronan, Killodiernan and Liathmore).

The penultimate doorway example in this group is in the Round Tower at Kildare (**77**). This rather defaced opening (**78**) has classic chevron decoration of the post-1130 period. On its exterior are fragmentary remains of a contemporary pediment or gable. This worked as an elaborate hood to keep water from dripping down onto the doorway, but it presumably also had symbolic value, and the space inside it may well have been painted or have contained some sculpture. Six Irish Romanesque churches, ranging in date from *c.*1130 (Cashel) to *c.*1180 (Clonfert), have simple pediments over their doorways. The pedimented church doorway which is nearest geographically to Kildare is at Killeshin, about forty miles south. It dates from the middle of the twelfth century, and this is a reasonable date for Kildare also.

76 *The doorway of Dysert Oenghusa Round Tower, showing the slight remains of pellet ornament*

77 *The Round Tower at Kildare. Not for sale!*

78 *The twelfth-century Romanesque doorway of Kildare Round Tower with its fragmentary pediment*

79 *The twelfth-century Romanesque doorway of Timahoe Round Tower*

Finally, we come to Timahoe Round Tower, which has the finest of the doorways (**79**). Its various decorative devices – including heads or faces – are typical of what one finds on contemporary church doorways across the centre of Ireland. Although unpedimented, the closest parallel is again at Killeshin, about twenty miles to the south-east, and this suggests that Timahoe is a work of *c*.1150.

The remainder

More than half the towers – a proportion exaggerated by the presence of some very fragmentary remains – are undatable. The problem is that lintelled openings for doors or windows cannot be dated accurately, nor can round-headed windows or doors in which the arch is monolithic. If we follow the principle that towers which possess lintelled or monolithic-arched openings reflect a simple unavailability to their builders of ideas of alternative forms, we may be looking at tenth- or early eleventh-century towers at Antrim, Castledermot, Clondalkin, Clones, Kinneigh, Lusk, Roscam and Swords (**33**, **34**). These are all plain towers, though Antrim's starkness is relieved by a sculpture of a small cross above its doorway, a feature which can be paralleled on church doorways but which cannot actually be dated except generally to before 1130 (**80**).

This latter list is very interesting because it features a cluster of sites around Dublin and more specifically within *Dyfinnarskíri*, the hinterland of the Hiberno-Norse town. The Scandinavian settlers in the Dublin area were Christianised in the second half of the tenth century, and Dublin had its first bishop in the 1030s. Whether this sequence is relevant to understanding the ecclesiastical architecture around Dublin is not clear: the presence of early (i.e. later eleventh-century) examples of nave-and-chancel churches within the general region (**81**) may reflect influence from Dublin, not otherwise obvious because, apart from the crypt of its cathedral, so little remains of the city's pre-Norman Christian architecture. Tower-building in the region may simply be unconnected with the Scandinavian presence. We can use the Round Tower at Clondalkin (**82**), located in a small historic village which has been thoroughly gobbled up by Dublin's suburban expansion, to make this point.

The annals are silent about Clondalkin between the years 940 and 1071. Either side of this lacuna, however, the Uí Rónáin held secular and ecclesiastical power there, if discontinuously. They were present from the 860s, having removed 'foreigners' from Clondalkin's vicinity, and they were expelled after 1076 on the grounds that they were, by then, in illegitimate possession of the abbacy. On their expulsion, they were compelled to grant a church with land

80 *Lintelled doorways with crosses.* Left to right: *Antrim Round Tower; Fore church; Clonamery church (not to scale)*

81 Above *Reefert church at Glendalough, built* c.*1100 though largely rebuilt to appear as it does today in the 1800s*

82 Left *Clondalkin Round Tower*

and animals to the Céile Dé, a group of reforming clerics. The church in question may well be a small nave-and-chancel church which was excavated by Etienne Rynne in 1964; its architecture is consistent with what little we know of eleventh-century architecture in the Dublin/Glendalough area. The Round Tower presumably existed by 1076, in part because the Céile Dé did not build towers and in part because, as we will see below, the Round Towers do seem to be associated with the type of secular lordship which the Uí Rónáin possessed at Clondalkin. A pre-1076 date for the Round Tower is probably not inconsistent with its rather spartan architecture, but where between the 860s and the 1070s should we pitch it? Clondalkin sums up the problems we have with dating so many of the Round Towers.

3
Bells, processions, deaths
Round Tower functions

'Continuity' is a much-used but under-theorised term in archaeology. It is a concept which communicates the idea of unchanging cultural practices through time-periods in which change might be expected. One sometimes has the impression in archaeological writing that 'continuity' in ancient cultural practice amounts to a form of stasis, that it is about a lack of development brought about through cultural isolation, or a poverty of imagination, or physical and mental laziness. Such a judgement of any aspect of medieval Christian Ireland would certainly be unwarranted. The fact that the Round Tower 'lived' without significant alteration through two golden ages of Irish artistic culture – the tenth century and the twelfth century – makes it clear that its continuity of design was rational and deliberate. In this and the following chapter we will explore the idea that in the tenth century the Round Towers that began this long-lived sequence represented the marriage of a range of symbols and ritualised practices with a particular architectural principle.

Listing functions
The annals are our principal guides in trying to establish what functions Round Towers served. It may seem that we are splitting hairs here, but the annalists themselves did not *specifically* record what the towers were used for. Yes, they had a category name for them – they called them 'bell-houses' – and we take it from this that bell-ringing was the principal activity carried out inside them, but nowhere do the annalists imply that we should think of this being the *only* activity associated with the towers. Indeed, the annalists' testimonies of events in and around the towers provide hints of multifarious functions, and if they had not used the term bell-house we might not even put bell-ringing at the top of that list.

In this chapter we will examine that bell-ringing activity, and speculate on its purpose. We will then look at that widely known matter of fatalities within

83 *The Round Tower on Inis Cealtra*

towers, and consider how recorded deaths may illuminate a second function of these buildings, that of protection. Out of these two core issues, bell-ringing and death, we will construct a model of Round Tower usage.

The evidence that relics were destroyed in towers suggests a third function, which is that they were treasuries. This will be discussed here *inter alia* rather than as a heading in its own right.

A fourth suggestion is that they were look-out points, but we will not entertain this possibility seriously. At places like Kilkenny one can certainly see today the attraction of this suggestion (**colour plate 15** *top*), but the towers originally had caps rather than parapets, and their bell-storey windows, facing as they did the cardinal directions, did not really accommodate this function. Sometimes those windows were just too small or narrow anyway (**colour plate 15** *bottom*). Anyway, the principle of the look-out tower is that one can survey all points on the horizon, not just the cardinals.

A fifth suggested function, and one that is often encountered in general books on historic Ireland or in the guided tours of sites with Round Towers, is that these buildings were monastic status symbols. This is the most difficult of the suggested functions to actually say anything about. We will return to the 'monastic' part of this explanation later in this chapter. The 'status symbol' part is a rather lazy, throwaway, under-theorised one, and its proponents are probably guilty of confusing two very different ideas: status as reflected in the building of a tower and status as symbolised by a tower. The former is acceptable, insofar as we understand status to equate with political power and resourcefulness, but the latter is unacceptable as an explanation. Whatever Round Towers symbolised, it was presumably something more tangible than this.

Before proceeding, it needs to be stressed that not all towers necessarily adhered to the same basic principles of use. The primary uses of Round Towers when they first appeared may have been adhered to at sites of particular importance, however one measures importance, but there may be towers that were erected in imitation and in places where circumstances did not actually require them to be built. Just because, to use an analogy, kings and barons built stone castles after the eleventh century, it does not follow that every stone castle was built by a king or baron, and just because certain architectural arrangements in castles were devised for the domestic and ceremonial rituals of royal and baronial households, it does not follow that those same rituals were employed in every castle in which comparable architectural arrangements were employed. So, while a great tower like that on the Holy Island of Inis Cealtra (83) may have been built for a full range of ritual activities and with full understanding of the symbolism inherent in a building of its type, the same might not be true of a small tower like that on remote Tory Island. The explanations of Round Tower functions and origins which are unfolded below and in the following chapter are presented with this understanding. Ideas offered as explanations for the great towers, beginning perhaps with the lost tower of Armagh, should not be negated by virtue of seeming too far-fetched when offered as explanations of other towers.

Bells

The presence of bells is recorded only twice: in the destruction of Slane in 950 we learn that a prized bell – the 'best of bells' – was lost, suggesting that it was a bell with relic value or simply one of exceptional sonority, while several bells were destroyed when a fire destroyed a tower in Armagh in 1020. Presumably bells were rung in the towers' top storeys, their conical stone roofs providing fairly good acoustics and their cardinal-orientation windows allowing the sounds to leave the buildings.

84 Left *One of the carvings of an ecclesiastic from White Island, showing a crozier and a hand-bell.*
Right *An adaptation of a later tenth-century manuscript depiction from Spain of a bell-tower with hanging
bells with attached ropes*

Hand-bells or hanging bells?

We know little about the nature of the Round Tower bells themselves. Hand-
bells are commonly represented in early Christian sculpture in Ireland, often
appearing alongside staffs in the hands of saints or ecclesiastics (**84** *left*). Hand-
bells of saints made good relics; a sumptuous reliquary or shrine, now in the
National Museum of Ireland, was made in the early twelfth century to encase
St Patrick's bell. Over seventy actual hand-bells survive from the early Irish
Church, and they are small in size and made of sheet iron or cast bronze. These
bells seem to have been made before the appearance of the Round Towers in
the tenth century, so it is not possible to know if many, or indeed any, of them
saw action inside towers. One imagines that hand-bells used in Round Towers
would be rather battered from the experience, especially if the bell-ringer (or
aistreoir) held the bell in the splay of the narrow bell-storey window, but none
of the bells seems to have appropriate damage.

1 *The Round Tower at Monasterboice. The broken top of this tower may be a consequence of the late eleventh-century fire.*

2 Opposite: *The Round Tower at Clonmacnoise. The original top is missing: the present bell-storey and its windows date from the later Middle Ages.*

3 Above: *Duleek: the scar of a round tower which was incorporated in a square church tower in the late Middle Ages but has since disappeared.*

4 Top: *Devenish Island viewed from the lake, with the twelfth-century tower dominating the skyline.*
Above: *The base of the destroyed Round Tower at Devenish, in the shadow of the extant tower; is this the Round Tower in which the king of Fir Manach was killed in 1176?*

5 Opposite: *Meelick Round Tower and cemetery silhouetted against the evening sky.*

6 Top: *The Round Tower and cathedral at Kildare, viewed from the north-east.*
Above: *The Round Tower and cathedral at Cloyne, viewed from the north-east.*

7 Opposite: *The tapering Round Tower at Dysert Oenghusa. The church is late medieval in date but preserves early fabric.*

12 Above: *Dromiskin Round Tower doorway, showing a classic Romanesque recessed arch with missing angle-shafts, and two flanking but defaced heads.*

13 Opposite: *The west cross and the Round Tower at Monasterboice.*

14 Opposite: *Standing beside a fifteenth-century square church tower, the Round Tower at Swords has had its original upper portion replaced by a rather crudely built bell-storey.*

15 Top: *Tourists use the top of Kilkenny Round Tower as a vantage point. The small holes in the parapet above the bell-storey windows are later medieval drain holes, sole remnants of a remodelling with also included battlements.*
Above: *The cap of the Round Tower on the very exposed island of Scattery. If ever a tower needed to be used as a lookout this was it. But if ever a tower had windows ill-suited for watchmen to scan the horizon, this was it!*

16 Overleaf: *The turriform church at Earls Barton from the south.*

The chronology of surviving hand-bells, combined with the sheer physical labour involved in a bell-ringer ascending banks of ladders to ring a bell as many as seven times a day (to mark each of the daily offices), has led Roger Stalley to speculate that the bells which were used inside the towers were hung rather than held, and that they were operated by ropes dangling through the floors (which is how bells were rung later in the Middle Ages and into modern times). He has drawn attention to comparative evidence elsewhere from as early as the tenth century to support the possibility of hanging bells (**84** *right*). Such bells certainly make sense, and there were no technological barriers to making them at any stage between the tenth and twelfth centuries when the towers were being built. Moreover, in most cases the Round Tower floors were of timber, supported by set-backs in the wall-thickness or by corbels, so one can easily envisage a rope running from top to bottom through a series of perforations in the floors; it should be noted, though, that three towers – Castledermot, Meelick and Tory Island – had a simple internal vault each as part of its original fabric and that three other towers – Inis Cealtra, Kinneigh and Swords – originally had one flagged floor within. A twelfth-century reference to the work of a bell-ringer suggests that operating a bell in a *cloictheach* was more noble work than shaking a hand-bell, implying that the Round Tower bell was not a hand-bell. The sheer effort required to summon noise from a bell 30m up a tower by using a rope may have rendered it an especially meritorious action.

There are, alas, no surviving bells of a hanging type, nor any identified fragments of large bells or bell-casts of appropriate date in the archaeological collections. The reason may be that hanging bell metal was recycled, so that the Round Tower bells have been reincarnated in various other guises over the years. Hand-bell metal may have been recycled only rarely; maybe such bells had relic value, and that is why so many survive. There is no obvious structural evidence of a hanging frame of any sort inside any of the few towers which still stand to full height. Absence of evidence does not amount to evidence of absence, especially when so few of the towers have original masonry left from their caps, but it may be that the bells inside the towers were indeed hand-bells, as was always assumed to be the case. The 'several' bells lost in the tower in Armagh in 1020 would be consistent with this.

Ringing bells for the world outside

Why were bells rung inside Round Towers? The annalists are silent on this, but there are two general answers that one can give, and they are not mutually exclusive.

In the first, bells were rung with respect to activities *external* to the towers, such as mass in the main church. The towers, in other words, were built to simply facilitate a need to which their architecture was, in a sense, incidental. In this view, one might describe the towers as service buildings, like lighthouses, and even suggest that if the builders could have erected tall metal frames rather than stone drums to do the job they might just have done so.

The Divine Office is the most likely activity external to a tower for which a bell might have been rung. This Office – the daily cycle of prayers, psalms and hymns that runs at intervals from daybreak to dusk – has been a feature of western Christianity right from its very beginning. It was originally conceived for communal prayer, recitation and singing. Monastic communities are, and always have been, singularly well-equipped for such bouts of corporate worship, but in the early Church the Office was not exclusively monastic; rather, there was an expectation that 'ordinary' Christians would set aside parts of their day to such acts of devotion. We know little about such obligations in Ireland, but, drawing on evidence elsewhere, it is likely that by the time Christianity was well established here the expectations had shifted, or rather the burdens of participation among non-monastics had been commuted, so that our 'ordinary' Christians became spectators of prayerful rituals rather than active participants in them.

The point about introducing 'ordinary' Christians into the discussion is this: while Round Towers may have met the time-keeping and bell-ringing needs of monastic communities, they may not have fulfilled such functions exclusively for such communities. Round Towers were not, by necessity, monastic buildings. We will return to this point again below, when we consider the evidence for royal patronage of towers. Suffice it to say here that we cannot assume that a poorly documented church site which has a Round Tower was a monastic site.

One final comment before moving on is to acknowledge that most of the significant ecclesiastical sites in Ireland do seem to have had Round Towers but that there are certain key places at which none is recorded. There were towers at many of the places which were designated diocesan centres when the Irish Church's territorial organisation was restructured in the early twelfth century, for example, but there is an absence of towers or of any annalistic or anti-quarian records of towers at important diocesan centres like Clonfert, Lismore and Tuam. Many places with Patrician associations have towers, so the factors determining which sites had towers and which did not may have ancient roots in Irish Christianity.

Ringing bells for in-tower rituals

Round Towers may have been a little too elaborate for the bell-ringing activities inside them to have had exclusively external purposes. We must consider the second, rarely considered, possibility, which is that bells were rung with respect to rituals *inside* the towers. Bells could signal to those outside the key moments of in-tower rituals. The annalistic allusions to towers containing relics – and we must remember that annalists only tell us about relics in towers when they are stolen or destroyed – may be crucial here.

Relics and the cults which surrounded them were of enormous importance in the medieval Church: they represented tangible links with an otherwise intangible world, miracles were associated with them, oaths were sworn and justice meted out in their presence, and pilgrims came to venerate them. Sometimes the relics did the travelling: they were often brought on tour. We know from the eighth-century collection of Irish canon law that relics were customarily contained in altars, as would be appropriate to their sanctity. Certainly the storage spaces for relics, whether or not those relics were on display, were themselves spaces of sanctity during the Middle Ages. The fact of the loss of relics when (some) towers were wrecked indicates that relics were actually kept inside towers, and this in turn suggests that tower interiors contained sacred spaces or chapels, with altars. So, it is not unreasonable to think that some liturgical activities, like private or one-celebrant masses, were held in towers in the presence of relics, maybe on feast days or at key moments in the Church calendar.

We can speculate, then, that Round Tower interiors were places of liturgy, that they were possibly used on certain occasions, that the liturgical activities were probably focused on the upper storeys, and that access to tower interiors was restricted. Bell-ringing may well have marked whatever went on whenever relics were being moved in or out of the towers, or were prayed over inside the towers.

Doorways and windows: Round Towers as processional spaces

This suggestion that Round Towers contained chapels, or were themselves *de facto* churches, actually finds some support in the designs of their doorways and in the layout of their fenestration. Apropos of the former, we saw in the previous chapter that Round Tower doorways are marginally the most elaborate doorways in the corpus of generally plain doorways that we find in architecture of pre-1130 date in Ireland, and that newly built Round Towers after 1130 were often given quite elaborate doorways. These embellishments of the architecture at the points of entry amount to independent evidence that the interior spaces of the towers were sacred. The fact that one had to ascend a flight of steps in full view of the world to reach a Round Tower's doorway only reinforces this point (**85**). One imagines that a bell-ringer, important as he was, did not need a fancy doorway to give him access to a Round Tower interior, but a senior cleric entering a tower, relic in hand or mass in mind, possibly did. The elevated doorway would have given him an opportunity to stop briefly before entering the tower, to turn around to face those observing his actions, and to display his office, perhaps through holding a relic.

The (apparent) replacement in the twelfth century of original doorways at Kells and Donaghmore (**colour plate 10** *bottom left* and *right*) underscores this point. Indeed, in Donaghmore, and maybe also in Kells originally, there are heads flanking the jambs, suggesting that one entered between images of important persons, one of whom was presumably St Patrick. The carved

85 *The doorway of Monasterboice Round Tower, dating from the eleventh century; the metal stairs give an impression of how a doorway like this might originally have been accessed*

86 *The carving above the doorway of Donaghmore Round Tower, as photographed by Françoise Henry in the 1950s.* Photograph: Dept of Archaeology, UCD

figure above the doorway of Donaghmore has not elicited much comment, but it is a very curious figure indeed (**86**). The upper torso seems to belong to the crucified Christ; the head cranes forward in a manner that is not uncommon in Romanesque metalwork representations of Christ. The bottom part of the figure does not match the torso part very well, either in shape, carving style, or gesture: the feet are bent and turned to the right. There is enough curvature on the surface of the upper stone bearing the torso to suggest that it was made for display as part of the fabric of a Round Tower. But it is not inconceivable, however, that this stone was originally part of a crucifixion slab or a church doorway lintel, such as we can still see several miles to the south-east at Dunshaughlin (**87**), and that its surface was pared back to give it the curvature appropriate to use in a Round Tower. It is not inconceivable either that new hips and legs were provided when it was recycled for the tower in its twelfth-century incarnation.

Apropos of fenestration, it is striking how often the windows in the towers ascend clockwise. We noted this in the previous chapter. Liturgical and pilgrim processions followed clockwise routes, so it is possible that the windows of Round Towers were arranged to give the impression that our imaginary senior cleric, having entered the tower, was processing to its summit. In reality, he was climbing ladders, but to those outside the tower his ascent was seemingly clockwise and had windows to light its every stage. The bell may have signalled

87   *An ex situ lintel from a church at Dunshaughlin, showing the crucified Christ flanked by Stephanton and Longinus*

to the outside world his arrival at the upper storey. Clockwise processions, which were certainly not the preserve of senior clergy, had a long antiquity in the Irish Church by the time the Round Towers appeared, as witness their manifestations at Inishmurray and Glencolmcille, where local or national saints like Brigit and Patrick are among those who are invoked at altars by pilgrims. Ireland was not unique in having such pilgrim rituals. Late fifth-century and later pilgrims to the great church in Tours, a building we will meet again several times, could invoke St Martin's intercession by walking around the church towards the high altar and praying at certain locations, thus imitating what an inscription at the church's doorway described as St Martin's *sidereum iter*, his journey through the stars.

Processional activity of the type described here is almost as ancient as Christianity itself. To understand both its roots and its importance to the argument being constructed here about the Round Towers, we need to travel briefly to early Christian Jerusalem.

Jerusalem, pilgrimage, procession
The theatre of Christ's death and resurrection, Jerusalem, was the most potent of all the cities of Christian history. It was (and is, of course) as central to Judaism, and for a much longer period. An ancient Canaanite settlement, it attained Old Testament significance after the Israelite king David captured it in

the tenth century BC. David brought to it the Ark of the Covenant, the chest which contained the tablets on which the laws were inscribed. His son, Solomon, erected a temple or house at Jerusalem, and the ark, hitherto a portable object, was placed permanently in that temple's inner sanctuary. The city and temple were both destroyed by the army of the Babylonian king Nebuchadnezzar in the early sixth century BC and substantial numbers of its inhabitants were driven into exile. It was among those exiles that Jerusalem came to be identified as God's favoured place, as 'the centre of nations, with countries round about her', in the words of the prophet Ezekiel, himself an exile.

Ezekiel and Isaiah, another Israelite prophet in exile during the era of Babylonian power in Palestine, had written repeatedly of the repossession and building of a new Jerusalem, and of the building of a new temple there. When Palestine was finally reoccupied by the Israelites in the late fifth century BC the returned exiles struggled to subsist. The prophet Haggai attributed this to their sloth in rebuilding the temple. Clearly, then, rebuilding was a contract with God, and life itself depended on its terms being met. So, the city and temple were rebuilt.

This, though, was not the fulfilment of the prophesies. Both the city and temple were wrecked by the Romans in the first century of the Christian era. The Romans then established a new urban centre on the west side of the older city. The site of Christ's tomb was in the vicinity of this Roman settlement, and it had a Roman temple (dedicated to Venus) on it. When the emperor Constantine embraced Christianity at the start of the fourth century AD he ordered the demolition of the pagan temple. He ordered that the site itself be purified or sacralised, first by the removal of the stones and earth which had been contaminated by that temple, and then by its reconsecration. He then erected a new, magnificent, no-expenses-spared church, the Anastasis, with a great rotunda. Christ's tomb was now at the centre of a circular court formed of twelve circular columns with square piers at the cardinal points and roofed over with a dome (**88**).

From the third century, and possibly earlier, Jerusalem was the focal city of Christian pilgrimage around the places of Christ's life. It is clear from the testimony of Egeria, a Spanish pilgrim who recorded her experiences in Palestine at the end of the fourth century, that there were organised rituals of public prayer by pilgrims in the city and its environs by then. All of the actual sites which were associated with Christ had churches on them by that date, and these buildings were settings to which the pilgrims processed, cognitively re-enacting the passion as they went. The pilgrims then congregated in these buildings, engaging through liturgy with the key moments of Christ's last days. Such processions gave a tangible reality to the idea, expressed by Ezekiel and Eusebius and others, that Jerusalem was a sacred space: by moving prayerfully through the spaces between the holy sites, pilgrim processions rendered the

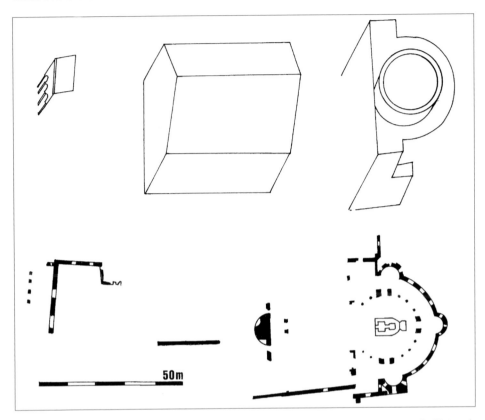

88 *The church of the Holy Sepulchre in Jerusalem: the bottom drawing shows the surviving early fabric and the top drawing shows a simple reconstruction of the superstructures (adapted from* La grammaire des formes et des styles: le monde chrétien, Bibliothèque des Arts *1982)*

city one vast holy site, a vast open-air church, with the Church of the Anastasis as its innermost sanctuary.

There was no corporeal relic in the middle of Jerusalem's sacred geography, no messianic body part at the centre of the spiritual choreography of pilgrimage. The martyrium built by Constantine was by far the most important martyrium in Christendom, but it contained no human remains. Its significance resided, somewhat ironically, in that very fact: it was a tomb with no body, precisely because Christ had been resurrected. The most venerated object-relic from Christ's life was actually the wood which still survived from his cross, allegedly discovered by Constantine's mother; relics of the True Cross, as we describe it now, were of course hugely valued right through the Middle Ages. The holy places themselves assumed the importance of relics, since these were places 'where [Christ's] feet stood', as Bishop Paulinus of Nola expressed it. The veneration of Christ was not confined to static relics associated with a static Christ: that act of processing, of perambulating and praying in recognition, even imitation, of Christ's passion, was itself an act of veneration. And so, just as a relic represented *translatio*, the translation of Christ's power into an inanimate object, so too could the pilgrim stations of Palestine be translated to new places. The holy places of Jerusalem could therefore be reproduced anywhere through the choreography and action of pilgrim procession.

The key monument of Christian Jerusalem, the Church of the Anastasis, stood at a distance from, but was still intervisible with, the ruined ancient temple, which was the key monument of Israelite Jerusalem. The symbolism of this geography was not lost on Eusebius of Caesarea, Constantine's biographer. He identified this as the 'new' Jerusalem of the prophesies, and he noted that it occupied a new site, facing the one 'renewed of old'.

The notion of a heavenly Jerusalem emerged with full force in the aftermath of the destruction of the rebuilt city and its rebuilt temple by the Romans in 70 BC. In addition to being a terrestrial city, Jerusalem was 'graven on the palms of [God's] hands', as Isaiah expressed it. The city thus had a dual reality in the minds of first-century BC writers: its survival on Earth, even in the face of such destructive forces as the Roman army, was guaranteed because God had already fashioned the city as an entity, had even shown it to Adam, Abraham and Moses, and would one day lower it into Palestine from the heavens. There are echoes of this perhaps at the dawn of the Christian era: Mark's gospel tells us that Jesus, who had famously driven money-changers from the temple, promised in his trial before the Romans to 'destroy the temple that is made with hands' and to 'build another, not made with hands'. In the era which followed Jesus's death the understanding of the heavenly city appears to change: still the celestial twin of the terrestrial city, it emerges in the New Testament Book of Hebrews as the after-death destination of Christians, a place which does not descend to Earth from the skies but one to which the souls of the deceased travel.

Celestial Jerusalem existed in the scripture, terrestrial Jerusalem existed in the real world, far away from Ireland. But it was known about in Ireland. *De locis sanctis*, a late seventh-century account of the holy places of Christ's life by the Gallician bishop Arculf was available, having been edited by Adomnan, the abbot of Iona and biographer of St Columba. When we see early Irish Church sites with their multiple churches and altars, we may be looking at the attempted replication here of those (unseen) holy places of Palestine; when we observe modern pilgrims retracing the steps of medieval pilgrims at early church sites in Ireland we may be looking at a very deeply embedded *translatio* of the processions which Egeria observed sixteen centuries ago.

Returning to the Round Towers, there is some sense in the idea that the clockwise ascent of the windows was intended to communicate to people on the outside that privileged individuals inside the towers were processing upwards, or ascending, towards treasuries and their relics, and that in doing so they were re-enacting the *iter* or journey which originated in early Christian Jerusalem. We might interpret the raised doorways as part of this choreography.

It is possible to think of the towers, then, as churches in which the sanctuaries (the chancels, if you like) were at roof level, their elevation inherently symbolic, and their symbolism reinforced by the act of ascending to them. It is possible to think also that the in-tower rituals involving relics had their key moments revealed to those outside through the use of bells. One need only recall how, before the Second Vatican Council, a Roman Catholic priest performed the liturgy of the Eucharist with his back to the congregation and how a bell was rung at its key moments: the performance of the ritual was not seen, thereby remaining mysterious, so the sound of the bell was effectively its surrogate.

Can we reconcile this suggestion about the Round Towers as processional and liturgical buildings with the annalists' insistence that they were 'bell-houses'? Well, one could repeat that the annalists did not insist that the towers were *only* bell-houses, but that *cloictheach* was a moniker which acknowledged a particular use or activity. Better still, we could translate the *teach / tech* element as meaning 'church', as is entirely permissible within a medieval Irish Christian context: after all, the term for a timber church was *dairthech*, meaning a 'house' of oak, while small relic-bearing churches to founder saints sometimes also possess the 'house' element, as for example at St Declan's 'house' (**68**), towards which the Round Tower at Ardmore actually faced. A famous example of a 'tomb-church' is *Teampall Chiaráin* at Clonmacnoise (**89**). Perhaps the annalists were really telling us all along that these were bell-*churches*!

Royal money, royal death

The annalistic record makes it clear that an attack on a tower by natural or human forces was likely to result in the loss of objects, or people, or both. The loss of objects like relics may have been of greater long-term import for any community in the Middle Ages, except when the numbers of human fatalities were huge, but it is the loss of life that has created the biggest headlines about these towers, nourishing the presentations of tour-guides ever since. As with the bells, we can spin some speculation out of these references to fatalities.

The unnamed dead
Fatalities in towers fall into two categories. First, we have unnamed or unranked persons who die together and in large numbers. There are actually only two recorded instances of such fatalities, both in Meath: Trim in 1126 or 1127, and Tullaghard in 1171. The prose of the annalists is matter-of-fact; modern minds have divined from these brief written accounts that the towers were jammed with people huddled in terror, hoping that the buildings would keep them safe. These events are the principal source of the popular view of Round Towers as places of refuge and self-protection.

89   Teampall Chiaráin *at Clonmacnoise, with Temple Finghin in the background.*

How real is this view? The fact that these buildings are towers and had bells rung from inside them is very interesting with respect to this question. 'Belfry', which is a word often used synonymously with bell-tower, comes from the Middle English *berefrey*, meaning a secure or protected place. The idea of a belfry as a protective structure is suggested as early as the fifth century when the bell-tower at the west end of the church of St Martin at Tours (the same church as was mentioned above) was described as 'security for the timid but an obstacle to the proud'. Here 'security' was presumably meant metaphorically. The belfry as a defensive structure or appendage is also attested in late Anglo-Saxon England: there was a 'wooden belfry 140 feet high' at a lord's residence at Cockfield, and here too the protection may have been symbolic rather than real. Interestingly, though, a belfry was also a type of medieval siege machine used in castle warfare – it was that large, wheeled tower, covered in animal skins, so beloved of adventure film makers!

Notwithstanding the *berefrey*, the reality is that Round Towers were not actually equipped for defence other than in the most passive sense. The elevation of their doorways made them difficult to enter, but that was the practical limit of their defensibility. In fact, Round Towers were really death-traps; with timber floors, narrow windows, and no means of exit except through the one small door, the killing of occupants by fire or asphyxiation was relatively easily achieved. Perhaps ironically, the high visibility of Round Towers may have shortened the odds on a church site being attacked, especially by 'foreigners' – the term is borrowed from the account of Slane in 950 – unaware of the local ecclesiastical geography. One church site which was attacked several times by such foreigners was Scattery Island, located in the Shannon estuary, and its Round Tower, which conveniently announced the site's existence to every mariner heading for Limerick and beyond, was singu- larly ill-equipped for the protection or even short-term comfort of occupants (**90**). Common sense suggests that church communities and the laity around them would have scattered in advance of an attack, and that Round Towers were an option of last resort, unless, of course, the refuge sought in them was of a particular type: sanctuary.

Since late Antiquity unarmed persons within the Empire had constitutional rights, protected by imperial imprimatur, to sanctuary within a church. The same principle – that earthly laws are suspended within consecrated spaces – is historically attested in the early Irish Church, where the *termonn* (derived from the Latin *terminus*) defined the sanctified space within which stood the church and later the Round Tower. Theft, assault, or murder within this space invoked the wrath of the saint. However, as soon as the annals begin to record the existence of church buildings they also begin to record violent deaths inside churches. From the Viking Age on there are occasional mass fatalities on a shocking scale, and not all of them were perpetrated by Vikings: 260 were killed within the timber church at Trevet in 850, 150 were killed in another timber church at Drumraney nearly a century later, 200 were killed in the stone church at Ardbraccan in 1031 (with an unspecified number killed at the same place in 1115), 180 were killed in the stone church at Lusk in 1089, and 100 were killed in the timber church at Killeshin in 1042. We cannot say if these killings were of people who had gathered innocently inside churches for mass, or of people who had been rounded up inside the churches and then killed, or of people who had unsuccessfully sought spiritual refuge – the protection of God and of the saints – within the most sanctified space of all, the church. But given the numbers of people involved, the latter seems the most likely. Unfortunately for these people, churches did not always provide that sort of protection. Unfortunately for us, the annalists do not tell us the occasions on which they did.

The idea that Round Towers could have been places wherein sanctuary might especially be hoped for presupposes that these were consecrated buildings. It is a reasonable supposition. As we have argued, the presence within them of relics, and by extension altars, would tend to suggest as much, as would the special embellishment of their doorways.

Dead kings

The second category of fatality is more interesting still. We saw in the list of annalistic references that there are several cases in which people of rank are killed. Senior Church officers were killed at Slane and Fertagh; one has the impression

90 *The Round Tower on Scattery Island, showing the doorway at ground level and its very tiny, indeed barely visible, windows*

that in both cases they were in amongst many other people, so that their rank was almost incidental to their fate. But in two instances neither the rank of the deceased nor the setting of the crime seems to be incidental. These are the two royal deaths, exactly a century apart, at Kells in 1076 and Devenish in 1176.

In the latter case, *Domhnall son of Amhlaoibh Ó Maoil Ruaanaidh, king of Fir Manach, was burned by his own kinsmen in the cloicteach of Daimhinis*. One might envisage here a king fleeing his kinsmen and hoping that the tower might hide him or protect him. Alternatively, one might view the tower as the place chosen for his execution, with the burning of the tower sealing his fate; it is a scenario which will remind some readers of the fate of the policeman at the climax of *The Wicker Man*! The annalists clearly attached importance to the venue of this killing. They do not tell us what happened to the tower after-wards, but they may have assumed their readers knew that a tower which is burned is a tower which will fall. One wonders if this crime scene should be identified as the Round Tower foundation in the shadow of the near-perfect tower at Devenish today (**colour plate 4** *bottom*): a date after 1176 for the latter would not be unreasonable, so we could suggest that it was built to replace the one in which Domhnall died.

In the case of Kells, *Murchad, son of Flann Ua Maeleachlainn, at the expiration of three days and three nights after his having assumed the supremacy of Teamhiar, was treacherously killed in the Cloicteach of Ceannus, by the lord of Gailemga, Amhlaeibh, the grandson of Maelan; and the latter was himself immediately slain in revenge, through the miracles of God and Colum-Cille, by Maelseachlainn, son of Conchobhar.* Here, again, the tower (**5**) was certainly more than a passive backdrop for an act of extreme violence. We do not know the circumstances under which the king was in the tower, but the fact that his killing is described here as treacherous indicates that he was taken by surprise, and that in turn suggests that he was there in connection with some action or duty associated with his kingship. When the annalists tell us that the killer was himself killed in revenge 'through the miracles of God and Colum-Cille', one wonders if the location of his deed was a factor in generating this vengeful miracle.

That Round Towers should ever be associated with kings in the annals is important. Kells and Devenish are not the only examples: we know from Clonmacnoise that the completion of the Round Tower in 1124 was assisted by Toirrdelbach Ó Conchobhair, king of Connacht, and we will speculate below that Cashel's Round Tower was built under the patronage of Muirchertach Ua Briain, king of Munster. The annals are generally silent about acts of construction; if they told us more we might well find that royal patronage of Round Towers was quite common. At the very least, the evidence from these few sites suggests a greater royal involvement in the Round Tower phenomenon than the older, monastery-oriented, view of these buildings would allow. Attacks on church sites with Round Towers, few as they were, might also be explained in terms of those sites' royal connections.

91 *The Anglo-Saxon church at Earls Barton overlooks an open area in the centre of its associated settlement*

Let us turn for a moment to later Anglo-Saxon England to develop this point about royal patronage. It is surely significant that square *tower-churches* (as distinct from *church-towers*) here, like Earls Barton (**colour plate 16**), dated by David Parsons to the earlier tenth century or before, were products of secular lordship, often located in enclosed residential sites or *burhs* and often associated also with territorial or estate boundaries. These very churches may also have contained bells: the later documentary sources on which we depend for their interpretation specify the importance of a bell-church or bell-tower as part of the package of structures that made up a *burh*. Some of the square tower-churches, like Debenham, Wickham and Earls Barton itself, have upper-level doorways which seem to have looked out on the landscape (**91**). From here, framed as if standing within a Classical aedicule, the thegn or lord could survey the estate and be seen doing so. The elevation of the doorway is critical here. Notwithstanding the morphological differences, the parallels with what we find in Ireland is striking.

We speculated earlier about senior clerics ascending to the high doorways of Round Towers and stopping briefly to display themselves and relics before proceeding to imitate a procession within. Bearing in mind the Anglo-Saxon tower-churches, is it possible that Irish kings did the same thing, using the relics to legitimise their kingship and to display their essential bond with their Church? Did royal money help finance the towers for these very purposes? Was

Murchad's presence inside the Kells tower at the moment of his death precisely because it was as much a project of his family as a building of the monastery? He was certainly not in there to ring a bell. Was Domhnall deliberately killed inside a tower that he himself had funded at Devenish? Is that the reason his kinsmen burned the tower as well as him?

The suggested connection of the Round Towers with royal patronage does not undermine the suggestions made in the previous section about how the towers functioned. The ritual uses of towers, for which bell-ringing was a crucial sonic element, did not preclude royal involvement. Local secular powers could have participated in such rituals. Royal patrons may have felt towers were value for money: towers allowed them to edge their way on to church sites and into church rituals, and towers may have allowed them – figuratively speaking, of course – to 'play Charlemagne' by positioning themselves in the upper opening, as the great emperor did in his great church at Aachen. Perhaps in building towers which faced the four corners of the world and marked the passage of time for the Divine Office, kings were taking control of time itself.

Cashel: a case-study in the politics of royal patronage

Let us finish this discussion by turning to the most spectacularly sited of all Round Towers, that on the Rock of Cashel (see **67**). This great natural outcrop had been the centre of secular power in Munster during the early Middle Ages. A natural choice for a citadel, it was given particular potency by virtue of an origin tale in which it is revealed in a vision to a chosen individual as a sacred rock or mountain. Thus it fits a universal pattern. Elevated religious or quasi-religious sites around the world have similar notions – one might even say cartographies – of other-wordly origin attached to them. Ezekiel portrayed Jerusalem in such terms, locating it on 'a very high mountain' (ignoring the fact that it is overlooked by even higher ground!) and suggesting a gradation of sanctity as the ground fell away.

Anyway, in 1101 the king of Munster, Muirchertach Ua Briain, a member of a dynasty with no ancestral connection to Cashel, granted the Rock to the Church in perpetuity. It was a pious gift of enormous import: it underscored his dynasty's ecclesiastical credentials at a key moment in the history of the Irish Church (the birth of an indigenous reform movement in the tradition of the Gregorian reform), and it also deprived the rival Mac Cárrthaig dynasty the possibility of re-establishing themselves as secular powers on their own ancestral site.

A new cathedral was built by the Church after 1101. It is now gone, replaced by successive Gothic rebuilds. A Round Tower was also built to the north-west of this cathedral, its doorway facing the original cathedral's doorway, and

92 *The summit of the Rock of Cashel from the east, showing the Round Tower on the right and Cormac's Chapel on the left, both dwarfed by the bulk of the thirteenth-century and later cathedral.*

Cormac's Chapel was built to its south-west (**92**). We know the patronage of the latter: it bears the name of its patron, Cormac Mac Cárrthaig, and has done since the Middle Ages. What about the Round Tower?

The consensus among scholars has long been that Muirchertach was its builder, and that its construction took place between 1101 and his death in 1119. The tower's architecture – it has an architraved round-arched doorway – is certainly consistent with this chronology, as we saw in the previous chapter, and Muirchertach's authorship fits with what little we know about tower builders. In the light of what was argued above, one could argue that Muirchertach's patronage of the bell-tower or bell-church was guided not by his desire that the cathedral chapter would wake in time for mass and the Divine Office but by the political sub-text which, it is argued here, Round Towers uniquely possessed. In other words, Muirchertach gave the Rock to the Church as a pious gift and then, almost surreptitiously, located himself and his dynasty on the Rock through the building of a Round Tower beside the cathedral.

93 Left *The pyramidal roof of the square-shaped north tower of Cormac's Chapel, viewed from the crossing tower of the adjoining cathedral*

94 Opposite *A cross section looking north of Cormac's Chapel with the north tower, which is behind this section and should not therefore be visible here, projected forward in outline to show (a) how it relates to the church's interior and (b) the scale of the doorway exiting from it into the nave*

In 1127 King Cormac Mac Cárrthaig, who had restored the ancient dynastic power to Cashel, seems to have addressed this challenge of the Rock now being in the possession of the Church by erecting a royal chapel of his own. His eponymous chapel is Ireland's most magnificent Romanesque church. Cormac built this two-storeyed, stone-roofed church on the opposite side of the cathedral from Muirchertach's Round Tower, and he put its main doorway facing a newly erected High Cross in the open space in front of the cathedral.

Two features of the chapel are of special interest here. First, its plan was a little asymmetrical: relative to the central axis of its chancel, its nave was a little more extensive on its north side than on its south. Secondly, it was provided with two tall towers on each side of the east end of its nave; we know that clerics from the Irish Benedictine monasteries of southern Germany were in

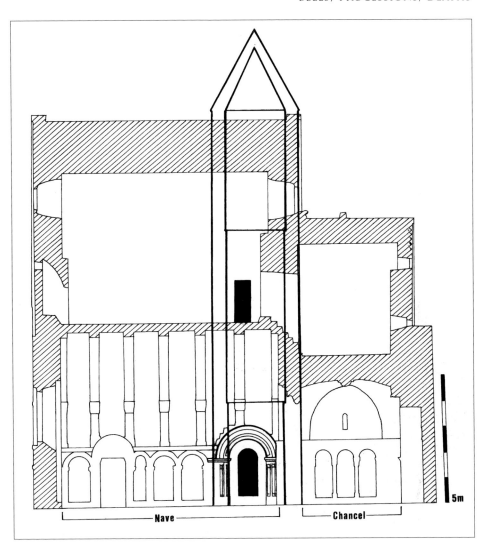

Nave — — Chancel — 5m

Cashel in the early 1100s, so it is likely that the paired towers were built in emulation of the types of tower which one finds in Romanesque churches of that region. Despite its square plan, the north tower of Cormac's Chapel was quite like a conventional Round Tower in two respects: it had timber flooring throughout and it was capped by a pyramidal roof (93). These two observations, plus the fact that the doorway connecting this tower with the small nave of the chapel is extraordinarily elaborate (94), and that the north side of the nave is a little more spacious, suggest to me that Cormac may have shifted whatever ritual activities were associated with Muirchertach's Round Tower into his chapel. Surely it is no coincidence that a fragment of the crest of a bell-shrine was recovered from the roof space above the chapel's nave!

4

Where did the Round Tower *idea* come from?

We do not know what the very first towers looked like, so we do not know for certain if the Round Tower 'arrived' in Ireland as a fully fledged monument type, or if it was the product of some architectural evolution on the island from, say, long-lost towers of significantly lower height, or even square towers. But the apparent consistency of design over the period represented by the standing towers does suggest very strongly that the earliest towers were the same as the latest, that they were as they appear today right from the very outset. Moreover, a late eighteenth-century drawing of the tower at Downpatrick, presumably the same (tenth-century?) tower as mentioned by the annalists as having been struck by lightning in 1015/16, shows a tall structure of fairly classic type (**95**). This surely removes the possibility – a very unlikely one, anyway – that the Irish Round Tower is entirely an invention of the Irish, whose architectural inventiveness is conspicuously underwhelming, made without significant reference to architecture elsewhere. At the same time, there must have been some level of invention: the absence of exact comparanda elsewhere that might be identified as models for those first towers indicates that Irish builders worked imaginatively off some template elsewhere in the Christian world. That template was not just stylistic; Round Towers were not built because they looked nice. Rather, the template must have had functional and iconographic appeal to the Irish.

But should we talk about template here in the singular or in the plural? Probably the latter: templates. And that is what makes the search for Round Tower origins so difficult.

We can locate various formal and conceptual comparanda for the Irish towers in parts of medieval Europe, and we will see some of these below. We have already encountered some: in Anglo-Saxon England there are the turriform (or tower-) churches like Earls Barton and the thegnly belfries as at Cockfield. Anglo-Saxon England also has square towers (with belfry windows facing the cardinal directions) positioned at the west ends of churches, espe-

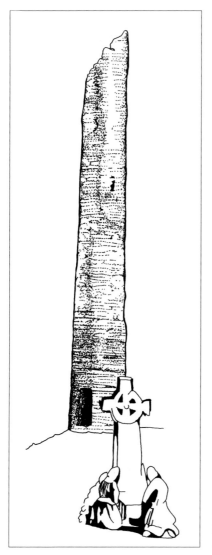

95 *The Round Tower at Downpatrick, adapted from a painting (in the National Library of Ireland) by Charles Lilly, 1790*

cially in eastern and northern England, and circular towers with similar windows and similarly attached to churches in, mainly, East Anglia; the towers of these two groups are traditionally identified as immediately pre-1066 in date but many certainly fall within the early Norman period.

When we look at these various towers, as well as church towers elsewhere in Europe, we know that they have relevance to the Irish Round Tower story on account of their common formal and conceptual aspects. But their relevance is often as parallels rather than as progenitors: in other words, they share with the Irish towers some common sources or group of sources, but they are products of different lines of development. So, we do not need to accommodate *all* parallels for the Irish towers, wherever they are found in

Europe, in our account of Irish Round Tower origins and development. On the contrary, our challenge is to separate the parallels from the possible progenitors. The English towers, most of which post-date the first Irish towers, are clearly parallels, so they may provide useful hints about where we should be looking for ultimate Round Tower origins, but they are not part of our story. Somewhere in among the towers of Carolingian Europe (the Europe of Charlemagne's empire in the 800s and 900s) or of the Mediterranean lands may be those actual models on which the Irish drew.

Formal origins: towards a working hypothesis

The Irish Round Tower is precisely that: Irish. Apart from two very close cousins in Scotland, at Abernethy and Brechin, and one on the Isle of Man, at Peel, it is *sui generis*: it has distant relations across Europe but it possesses a unique physiognomy. It is as instantly identifiable as Irish as, say, the decorated stave church is Norwegian. Not surprisingly, there is something of a scholarly industry surrounding the question of Round Tower origins, and its wheels have been spinning for more than a century. Two areas have emerged among scholars as the principal contenders: the Mediterranean, particularly Italy, and west-central Europe north of the Alps, which embraced areas of the early medieval Carolingian and Ottonian empires. The theses which identify either of these areas as source areas acknowledge the importance of bell-ringing as a common functional denominator with the Irish towers, but thereafter stress the *formal* comparisons which can be made: the towers in the three areas are tall and cylindrical, and their largest or at least the most numerous windows are at top-storey level.

The Mediterranean-origin thesis has in its favour the fact that there are some extant free-standing towers in that region, notably the brick-built towers in Ravenna, even if these are a little later than the earliest Irish towers. Thanks to Peter Harbison's research we also have illustrative clues about long-lost, free-standing, cylindrical *campanile* in Rome, Jerusalem and Antioch, possibly dating to the period before the first towers appeared in Ireland; incidentally, their battlemented parapets have led to the suggestion that we should look again at the possibility that such parapets in Ireland are actually original (**96, 97**), but in each case the evidence suggests the battlements are later than the towers.

Anyway, to return to the thesis of a Mediterranean origin, Rome was a popular destination for Irish pilgrims. We know that Irish clerics went to Rome in the early seventh century on business connected with the then-raging controversy over the dating of Easter, while conventional pilgrimage from Ireland to Rome had certainly begun by the ninth century and was relatively common – relative to the number of times that annalists mention pilgrims, that is – in the eleventh century. Jerusalem, further away at the eastern end of the

96 *The Round Tower at Castledermot*

Mediterranean, was less familiar ground to pilgrims from Ireland, but some knowledge of its holy places was available through *De locis sanctis*.

The other thesis emphasises the great likeness between the Irish *cloigthithe* (modern Irish) and the north European *cocleae*, the bell-towers with internal stairs which are physically attached, either in pairs or in pairs of pairs, to the great churches of the Rhineland and surrounding territories (**98**). Significantly, the *cocleae* which flank the 'westworks' of churches are often at the north-west and south-west corners, while the Irish towers, which are single, not paired, are normally located to the north-west or south-west of their associated churches. The chronology also works well for the north European thesis: towers first appear there in the tenth century, which is about the same time as they appear in Ireland. So too, albeit in a general sense, does the history work well: Irish missionary activity on the Continent is well documented, so it does not stretch the imagination to envisage the ideas travelling along routes already well-trodden by assorted holy men.

97 *The Round Tower at Cloyne*

98 *St Michael's, Hildesheim, from the south, showing the cylindrical bell-towers at both east and west ends*

In fact, historical context allows for a thesis of Irish Round Tower origins which combines the two theses outlined above. We know that Irish pilgrims to Rome invariably travelled via the Rhineland, thus bringing them into potential contact with all sorts of towers. So, just as the architectural traditions of the Carolingian empire owed a debt to late Antique and early medieval architectural traditions of the Mediterranean, not least with Charlemagne's palatine chapel in Aachen taking inspiration from San Vitale in Ravenna, built in the sixth century by Justinian, the Irish towers could conceivably owe a debt to buildings within both traditions.

We can construct, then, a fairly sensible working hypothesis of Irish Round Tower origins which accommodates both sets of parallels and enjoys the comfort of a general history of early medieval Ireland in its European context. This hypothesis runs as follows. Free-standing bell-towers are seen by pilgrims in Rome and their bells are heard. Their value as visual correlatives and acoustic amplifiers for an act which is already a feature of Ireland's Christian communities – bell-ringing – is understood there and then, as is the potential iconographic value back in Ireland of erecting buildings of Italianate origin. The idea is transmitted back to Ireland, along with its terminology, which will be translated to *cloictheach* when it lands here. Transmission is via the

Rhineland, where a particular architectural grammar for bell-towers has already been devised, and this grammar will inform the Irish towers' outward appearance, but the Irish towers will be detached from their associated churches, as per the Mediterranean models, and they will occur singly rather than in pairs, as per the original sources again.

This hypothesis has as its bottom line the identification of the Irish towers with bell-towers elsewhere. It is the same bottom line that informs all published attempts at identifying Round Tower origins, and to that extent it represents another variation, albeit a very slight one, on what other writers have suggested on this subject. There the matter can be left to rest until more detailed analysis of the various towers might illuminate the processes of selection and transmission a little more.

Conceptual origins: towards an alternative working hypothesis

But what happens when we introduce into this discussion those aspects of Round Tower usage on which we speculated in the previous chapter? Was it the case that the towers, once built, suggested to their builders that relics could safely be stored inside them? Would the preferred environment for the containment and maybe even the display of relics on many church sites between the tenth and twelfth centuries have been arrived at so incidentally, and without any significant alteration to the architectural language of the host buildings?

With these questions in mind, it is useful to step back from the debate for a moment to reflect on what exactly we should be looking for under this heading of 'origins'. We need, obviously, to think of mechanisms by which the ideas of form and function which are manifest in the Round Towers could have been transmitted to Ireland: uttering the word 'pilgrim' is really not enough. But our problem is more complex than that. We need to explain how and why certain elements or features of possible progenitors elsewhere might have been dropped or abandoned in any such transmission. Most importantly, we need to understand what it was about these towers that made them acceptable in the first place to Irish church-building communities that had conservative architectural tastes right up to the start of the twelfth century. A sudden realisation somewhere in early tenth-century Ireland that bells are best heard from elevated positions and that Italianate towers did the job very well is not an acceptable explanation, especially when one factors in those other functions which the towers fulfilled. To my mind, the Round Tower, while an imported idea of architectural structure and space, must have had some conceptual or ritual genealogy in the Irish Christian tradition both as a monument type and as a setting for certain ritual practices involving relics, processions and kings. If visually it represented a radical departure, its radicalism must have been offset by some functional or symbolic adherence to the existing practices or landscapes with which people in early medieval Ireland were familiar. The clockwise arrangement of windows in Round Towers, combined with the veneration of relics, suggest that the processional-devotional nature of the early Irish Church and its landscape manifestation provide that connection.

The Round Tower and the Holy Sepulchre

Developing from what has been said, I wish to suggest that Round Tower origins should not be sought among the formal designs of European bell-towers of the ninth and tenth centuries as has hitherto been done, but rather in the corpus of cognitive or symbolic architecture which has the Holy Sepulchre in Jerusalem at its core.

We have seen that the Irish Round Towers occur in association with churches; this was one of the planks on which the post-Petrie consensus was built. Sometimes there is just one church (as far as can be seen above ground, anyway), and it and the tower form a group of two buildings. Sometimes the towers are on sites where there are multiple churches, so they are a part of a larger group of buildings, but even here the tower and main church form a sub-group of two by virtue of the fact that the former faces the latter. This simple observation – that the Round Tower is an individual element within a group of free-standing monuments – may be crucial to understanding it. Why? There are two answers.

First, as a building which was physically separate from any other, the Irish Round Tower had both structural and functional integrity, and this must have had implications in the Middle Ages for how it was understood in and of itself, as well as in liturgical and spatial relation to the church. Because it stood in open space, the rituals associated with it involved some element of open display, and while any ritual activities inside the towers may have been mysterious, not least because the windows were so small, anybody intending on entering a tower as part of some routine did so in full view of others. This was not the case with towers attached to churches. So, to suggest that the Irish towers are modelled on Continental towers attached to churches is to fundamentally misunderstand them.

Secondly, and more importantly, if the towers were consecrated spaces, as was argued above, a single church and a Round Tower facing each other created a dual ritual focus (**99**). Once we conceptualise in this way the two buildings as one, some very interesting interpretative options light up.

Within the Carolingian and Ottonian worlds great churches had dual liturgical foci: one focus was at the west end, and was contained within a 'westwork' or large structural 'massif' several storeys high, and the other focus

99 *The Round Tower and cathedral on Scattery Island*

was located at the east end. The western focus was given over to celebrating Christ's passion and resurrection, a fact underlined by its common dedication to the Saviour. It evoked very explicitly the Holy Sepulchre, especially in those instances where it was of circular or cylindrical plan. This was famously the case in the Carolingian abbey church of *Centula* or St Riquier, now destroyed but known to us from its own documentary record and from an early – and much-disputed – drawing (**100**). Here the western tower had a *crypta Salvatoris* containing relics from Christ's life. Its open, three-storeyed, roof allowed light to stream into what was an upper chapel. Carol Heitz has shown how similar, open-roofed, cylindrical towers are used to represent the Holy Sepulchre on contemporary ivories, as in the case of the tenth-century ivory from the Carrand Collection in Bargello Museum in Florence (**101**) which shows the neatly rolled-up shroud in which Christ was wrapped stuffed into the lower stage of a cylindrical tower.

The western tower dedicated to Christ's passion and resurrection was not just a feature of the Carolingian or Ottonian world. It trickled down into the iconography of Romanesque churches within these same regions: towers such as those at St-Savin-sur-Gartempe (**102**) perpetuate the older scheme, even though they drop the cylindrical shape. It is not insignificant that apocalyptic

100 *The destroyed Carolingian abbey church of* Centula / St Riquier *as drawn in the early seventeenth century*

imagery drawn from St John's Revelation occupies the tympana of great Romanesque *west* portals at places like Moissac, or that when God is represented addressing Judah and the Israelites in the *c.*1100 Bible of St Martial of Limoges, he is depicted inside the upper storey of a tower (**103**).

The *Centula* scheme was not really an invention of the Carolingian age. The lost fifth-century church of St Martin at Tours, known to us from a contemporary account, is a clear formal progenitor, and is one of enormous interest for the study of the Irish towers. The west end of this church had a bell-tower, and displayed somewhere on it was a remarkable inscription for the penitent about to enter the building. It began with an invitation to the penitent to look up at the tower and note its loftiness. It then went on to proclaim the following: *This tower is security for the timid but an obstacle to the proud; it excludes proud hearts and protects the weak. That tower –* here the penitent was invited to look down the church at a second tower which was above the altar – *is higher. From there he who has already journeyed to the rewards of Christ calls people; having*

126

101 *The tomb of Christ as represented on a tenth-century Carolingian ivory, now in Florence*

gone on already, he has sanctified this journey through the stars. Having read this, the
penitent's journey through the church, or rather through the stars, towards the
high altar was signposted by frescoes and inscriptions, most of which seem to
have alluded to events in Martin's life. On the arch above the high altar and
beneath the tower was an inscription, *How this place must be feared. Indeed, it is
the temple of God and the gateway to heaven.* This latter inscription was drawn
explicitly from the Old Testament tale of Jacob's Ladder; Jacob had dreamed of
a ladder connecting earth and heaven, with angels going up and coming down,
and when he awoke and realised that the ladder ascended from the very spot

102 Left *St-Savin-sur-Gartempe from the east, showing the paired towers, the lower one over the crossing and the higher one (in the background) at the west end*

103 Opposite *God addressing Judah and the Israelites, from the second Bible of St Martial, c. 1100*

on which he had slept he proclaimed *How awesome is this place! This is none other than the house of God, and this is the gate of heaven.* So, while the route to heaven from the altar in St Martin's church was mystical, and came at the end of a journey imitative of St Martin's life through the church, the tower which rose over the altar acted as a physical, architectural, metaphor.

With these two examples, *Centula* and Tours, we have the raw material for an entirely different understanding of the Irish towers. The circular plan, the multi-windowed upper storey, and the presence of relics, not to mention the ladders, are consistent with the Irish towers being ritual spaces which evoked Christendom's greatest monuments and imitated their imagery. That evocation may have come through ninth-century northern Europe, which was the world

of *Centula*, the age and the place in which an architectural iconography appropriate to Jerusalem's universal importance was fashioned. The royal interest in Round Towers in Ireland can be explained in terms of both the imperial patronage of comparable exercises in architectural iconography in that region at that time, and the provision in great churches of open galleries which allowed dignitaries, like Charlemagne in Aachen, to look down at events below. Is it a coincidence that Charlemagne's famous chapel in Aachen had a diameter of 100ft – the measurement which we suggested above was optimal for the height of Round Towers?

Speculating on a direct Ireland-Mediterranean connection

In looking to Carolingian or Ottonian intermediaries for the Round Towers we may be overlooking the possibility of a direct Ireland-Jerusalem connection manifesting itself in this architecture, especially with regard to that spatial 'dialogue' between the Round Tower, which is *cylindrical*, and the associated church, which is *rectangular*.

The towers and churches constituted what was *de facto* a small 'church group'. Groups of churches are actually very common across early medieval Europe. The commonest grouping arrangement of churches in the Mediterranean (and in Gaul) in the earliest Christian period was of two churches, one a little larger than the other, and placed side-by-side or end-to-end, sometimes separated by a baptistery. The side-by-side pattern was especially common in the central and western parts of the Mediterranean while the end-to-end pattern was more common in the eastern Mediterranean. There were functional differences between the churches in these pairings: the larger church or *ecclesia maior* was generally used for festive or Sunday masses and for masses for the *catechumeni*, the children and converts who were undergoing Christian instruction, while the smaller church or *ecclesia minor* was the venue for the daily round of prayer (matins, lauds, vespers) and for masses for the *fideles* or neophytes, the already-baptised converts.

Most extant church groups in Ireland comprise buildings of tenth- and eleventh-century date and much later, but their general north-south pattern probably reflects ancient roots in Mediterranean practise. We know of two churches side-by-side in Armagh back in the seventh century. There may have been a similar scheme at Kildare: Cogitosus's famous seventh-century description of the church of the double monastery of Kildare specified an east-west partition separating men and women under the one roof, so the north-south division which is attested at Armagh is repeated here. Indeed, it is not inconceivable that there were at Kildare two conjoined churches rather than one church as we would conventionally understand it: where two churches constitute a group in the Mediterranean and in Gaul, that group invariably constitutes a cathedral complex in which both churches, together, are a part of the cathedral. When Cogitosus contrasted very deliberately this '*new* reality being born in an age-*old* setting' (emphasis added), it is tempting to think that he was alluding to the 'new reality' of Constantine's buildings in the 'age-old setting' of Palestine. It was not, in other words, a throwaway remark.

With the appearance of Round Towers in the 900s an east-west orientation of liturgical foci emerges in Ireland. We connected this above to the east-west arrangement of towers in Carolingian churches, themselves connected iconographically to the holy places of Christ's life. That remains, I think, the best solution to the question of Irish Round Tower origins, precisely because it combines structural form, function and architectural imagery. But is it possible that knowledge of the Holy Sepulchre itself was embedded in the creation of the Irish Round Tower? The Holy Sepulchre was a double-church with an east-west alignment; the Anastasis was its *ecclesia minor*, and the Martyrium its *ecclesia maior*. Not only does the *circular* tower and the *rectangular* church in Ireland replicate the circular Anastasis and its rectangular Martyrium, but that the Daily Office was observed in the circular component of the Holy Sepulchre may feed back into the suggestion that bell-ringing in the Round Towers was sometimes associated with the Divine Office.

5
Some closing thoughts

However remarkable they appear now, sometimes surrounded by ecclesiastical buildings of contemporary and later date, or sometimes standing as relatively isolated monuments, Round Towers must have seemed even more remarkable when they first appeared on the Irish landscape. Nothing in the earlier architectural tradition of the Irish Church – as far as we know, at any rate – approached them for technical sophistication or visual daring. The early Irish Church generally kept its head down on the rural landscape; it was a low-skyline Church. Elevated sites, deliberately chosen, gave many churches and monasteries a wide visibility, often in land of fairly good agricultural value, but the actual built structures had little elevation in themselves and they bear little evidence today that their builders were capable of construction at a larger scale. Round Towers first broke that pattern in the early 900s, and they continued to break it for two hundred years and more. It seems that it was not until the early 1100s, when Cormac Mac Cárrthaig built his chapel on the summit of the Rock of Cashel, that a stone building of comparable technical or visual bravado was erected in Ireland, and it is interesting to remember that Cormac's Chapel may have been built by masons with one eye on the older Round Tower at the same site.

Despite their great physical presence, the Round Towers have long been somewhat marginal in our thinking on ecclesiastical architecture and landscape in early medieval Ireland. Surprisingly, a spate of publications in recent years has not changed this. My book is a modest attempt to reinvigorate the discussion of Round Towers, first by reasserting how extraordinary is their architectural character when viewed alongside the other elements of the contemporary built environment, and secondly by suggesting that they were sacred rather than service buildings. A search for their formal origins brings us to northern Europe but ultimately to the Mediterranean. A search for their conceptual origins leads us into that world of medieval architectural iconography that had Jerusalem at its centre.

I would suggest that the Round Tower was *not* invented so that bells could be better heard. Indeed, I am not sure that it was invented to meet any particular need or range of needs. Its emergence – in Armagh? – might simply have been the outcome of a distillation of very complex ideas about procession and iconography by a Christian community which understood how these core issues in Christian practice were being monumentalised in contemporary European church-building. From the very beginning Round Towers were places of ritual activity involving relics. As buildings with formal and processional pedigrees reaching back to Jerusalem, Round Towers were an embodiment of the idea of *translatio*. And as buildings which drew on Carolingian, and ultimately Constantinian, models, Round Towers articulated the connection between secular and sacred power. The appearance of the first Round Towers about the same time as the great scriptural High Crosses (**104**) with their multi-layered iconography is probably no coincidence.

The Round Tower template created in the tenth century survived through three centuries, even if its initial *raison d'être* was not sustained to the very end. We can only speculate, but it is possible that its connection with kingship may well have taken centre stage by the eleventh century, which would explain our references to royal fatalities. It is possible also that sites without relics circumvented that problem by building Round Towers as surrogates, so the altar at the summit of a tower had special sanctity by virtue of its elevation and imitation. All the while, the annalists persisted with *cloictheach* whenever they had reason to mention one of these towers.

104 Opposite *The Cross of the Scriptures at Clonmacnoise, made at the start of the tenth century. The capstone here is shingle-roofed, rather like a small building (see also* **colour plate 13***). The capstones of some High Crosses, as at Ahenny most famously, are dome-like, and it has been suggested that they are modelled on Christendom's most famous building, the Holy Sepulchre in Jerusalem*

Gazetteer of Ireland's free-standing Round Towers

Aghadoe, Co. Kerry
A rural graveyard 6km to the north-west of Killarney, on the Killarney-Killorglin road.

This is a patched-together stump of what was originally a very fine tower. The original masonry was semi-ashlar, expertly laid in irregular courses with spalls (small in-fill stones) and dressed to the curve.

Aghagower, Co. Mayo
A village graveyard 7km to the south-east of Westport, off the Westport-Ballinrobe road.

The lower part, maybe even half, of this tower remains. The upper portion of the ruin, including a wide breach on the north side, was repaired about thirty-five years ago. The tower's masonry is roughly coursed and loosely jointed with spalls (small in-fill stones); many of the stones are long and flat. The original doorway, a couple of metres above present ground level, has a round arch, with the stones running right through the full thickness of the wall; there is a more recent doorway at ground level. The windows are lintelled.

Aghaviller, Co. Kilkenny
A small rural graveyard 3km south-west of Knocktopher, on the Kilkenny-Waterford road.

A once-fine tower, only the lower third or thereabouts now survives. It stands on a square base with an offset at ground level, a feature paralleled at Kilree several miles to the north. The masonry is semi-ashlar of consistent size, except at the top of the ruin where the stones are larger and more square-shaped; the masonry is laid in neat horizontal courses with larger stones used in the upper part of the remaining fabric. The original doorway, several metres above ground level, is round-arched. There is a second, later, doorway at ground level.

Antrim, Co. Antrim
The parkland grounds of Antrim Borough Council on Steeple Road in Antrim town.

This is a well-preserved tower of roughly coursed basalt, with granite used in the doorway and in the window surrounds. The top section of the tower has been restored, having been severely damaged by lightning in 1819. The doorway is a couple of metres above ground level. It has a lintel. The stone immediately above this lintel has a rounded top and carved on it in relief is a small ringed cross with a short shaft. It seems to be original to the tower. All the window openings in the tower are lintelled.

Ardfert, Co. Kerry
The graveyard of Ardfert Cathedral.

Barely visible traces of this tower can be detected among the graves to the south-west of Ardfert Cathedral. It stood until 1771.

Ardmore, Co. Waterford
A graveyard on the south side of the village overlooking the bay.

This tower is perhaps the most magnificent of the entire series. It is distinguished by three features. First, it has a most dramatic taper, its circumference decreasing by more than one-third from ground level to cornice. Secondly, there are three string-courses at different levels as its ascends; they break up the external surface of the tower but bear no relationship to the flooring inside. Finally, the masonry is ashlar, dressed to the curve, regularly coursed and consistently jointed throughout. The round-arched doorway, several metres above ground level, has a continuous roll-moulded surround; it also tapers from the sill to the arch. Angle-headed windows are used at belfry level. There are very worn bead mouldings on an upper-floor window. Corbels are distributed apparently randomly inside the tower; some of these have carvings of animal and human heads.

Ardpatrick, Co. Limerick

A rural, exposed, hill-top graveyard 8km south-east of Kilmallock, just off the Kilmallock-Kildorrery road.

Only parts of the lower walls of this tower remain. It was clearly a well-built tower: its stones are neatly squared off and dressed to the curve, and are laid in good horizontal courses. Much of the lime mortar has washed out and the joints have widened a little.

Ardrahan, Co. Galway

A village graveyard 12km north of Gort on the Limerick-Galway road.

The tower remains here are very fragmentary: incorporated in a graveyard wall are several courses of horizontally coursed and squared-off blocks of local limestone.

Armoy, Co. Antrim

A village graveyard, 11km south-west of Ballycastle on the Ballycastle-Ballymena road.

This tower stands to a little under half its original. It was built with largely undressed field stones and boulders laid in fairly regular courses with spalls (small stones) filling the interstices. The masonry changes character as the tower ascends: there are flat stones from the base to just above the doorway, with especially flat stones at doorway level, and more rounded cobbles towards the top of the surviving ruin. The very tall doorway, which seems to be original despite some irregularities in masonry, has a monolithic arch with a plain architrave which does not continue down the jambs. The interior of the tower was dug out in 1843 and assorted objects and human bones were found.

Balla, Co. Mayo

A small graveyard in the centre of the town, 13km south-east of Castlebar on the Castlebar-Claremorris road.

The lower part of a very fine tower of regularly coursed fabric; individual stone size increases markedly around the level of the upper doorway. The upper doorway is original: its lower jambs have roll-mouldings, so its plain or unmoulded upper jambs and its short lintel may be reused from a window higher up in the tower. There is also a pointed-arched doorway of a late medieval date at ground level.

Cashel, Co. Tipperary
The summit of the Rock of Cashel; the site itself is a heritage site with an entrance fee, but there is no access to the tower interior.

This is a complete Round Tower, incorporated into the north-east corner of the north transept of the Gothic cathedral; a thirteenth-century wall passage of the cathedral actually gave access to its interior. The tower stands opposite Cormac's Chapel, with that later cathedral now blocking the space between, and together they flanked the *platea* or open area in front of the original twelfth-century cathedral. The tower is well built, with semi-ashlar in fairly regular courses and dressed to the curve of the wall. There are small holes for scaffold poles throughout. The doorway is round-arched with voussoirs and architraved. The belfry windows are angle-headed.

Castledermot, Co. Kildare
A village graveyard 12km north of Carlow.

This is a most distinctive tower, constructed with rounded granite cobbles, largely uncoursed, with spalls (small infill stones). It stands as a complete tower now, albeit with a battlemented parapet rather than a conical roof, but the upper quarter, including the belfry windows, is an early modern rebuilding which is not faithful to the tower's original appearance. The doorway is tall and narrow with a lintel, and is slightly above modern ground level. There is a broken dome vault at a low level inside the tower and it seems to be original.

Clondalkin, Co. Dublin
The side of a modern road in a village which is now part of Dublin's south-western suburb.

This is a very fine and complete tower; it is also the narrowest of the entire series. Its fabric is local stone shaped roughly into regular shapes and laid with horizontal and vertical angles but in very irregular courses. Spalls (small infill stones) are used throughout. The doorway, of granite, is several metres off modern ground level and is now reached by a flight of stone steps which ascend on the side of a pronounced buttress-like feature at the tower's base. The buttress does not seem to contemporary with the tower but may be an early addition, possibly as a precaution because the tower's drum is quite slender; the steps might be later still, if only to judge by the anticlockwise direction in which they rise.

Clones, Co. Monaghan
A mainly seventeenth- and eighteenth-century graveyard in the centre of the town.

This is a nearly complete tower, lacking only its cap and part of its belfry floor. Its fabric, comprised of purplish stone which is roughly squared off and laid with spalls (small infill stones) in irregular courses, has a crumbly appearance thanks to unrecorded fire damage. The doorway and all the windows are lintelled.

Clonmacnoise, Co. Offaly
A heritage site with an entrance fee, but there is no access to the tower interior.

This is a very finely built tower as befits its location on one of Ireland's premier monastic sites. Its masonry is local limestone, cut as ashlar and laid in regular and well-jointed courses. The tower must have been quite a bit taller than it is today; the upper part that we see now is late medieval in date and it gives the tower an uncomfortably squat appearance. The doorway has a very finely wrought round arch with voussoirs and simple imposts. The original windows, however, are flat-headed.

Cloyne, Co. Cork
In the village opposite the cathedral; the village is 6km south of Midleton.

This is a very well-preserved tower, complete and untouched apart from at the very top where the original cone was replaced with a battlemented parapet in the late Middle Ages. The masonry is mainly of local, purplish, sandstone, which gives the tower a rather dark appearance. The stones are roughly squared but well coursed. The entrance doorway is lintelled but there is a large angle-headed window high up in the drum and facing in the same (eastward) direction.

Devenish, Co. Fermanagh
An uninhabited island 4km north of Enniskillen in Lower Lough Erne; access to the island is by local boat hire (including from Enniskillen), and there is seasonal access to the interior of the tower.

There were two towers here, one of which still stands as a complete building, and the other, beside it, remains only as a foundation. The complete tower – the recipient of conscientious repair in the nineteenth and twentieth centuries – is built with carefully coursed masonry, consisting of square and rectangular blocks neatly dressed to the curve of the wall. The doorway has a three-stone round arch with an architrave. Above the doorway is a large angle-headed window. The cornice separating the drum from the cap is decorated with scrolls and pellets and has four human heads (with interlaced beards of typical twelfth-century type) above the bell-storey windows.

Donaghmore, Co. Meath
A rural graveyard 4km north-east of Navan; follow the Navan-Drogheda road.

This is one of the more unusual towers in Ireland. It is exceptionally well built, with neatly squared-off local limestone laid in regular courses with some spalls. The doorway, which features two flanking heads and a Christ over the arch, is in sandstone and is possibly (*contra* George Petrie's firm statement) a replacement of an original doorway. Square-headed, angle-headed and round-headed window forms are represented in the drum. The cap survives, albeit repaired; the lack of a capstone or apex gives the tower a curious round-topped appearance. The most remarkable feature of the tower is the absence of windows at top-storey level.

Dromiskin, Co. Louth
A village graveyard, accessible via Castlebellingham, 3km south-east of Castlebelling-ham and 12km south of Dundalk.

This is a short, stumpy tower, built entirely of small rubble. It is of low height with large rectangular bell-storey windows and a low cap, but the bell-storey and cap are clearly later features. The tower's principal feature is its Romanesque doorway, with a recessed inner order (now missing) of detached columns. It probably dates from the early twelfth century.

Drumbo, Co. Down
A village graveyard 6km east of Lisburn; follow the Lisburn-Newtownbreda road.

This is the lower part of a tower, although its curious concave profile makes one wonder if it was ever significantly higher. It is built with very irregularly-coursed local slate, the mortar of which is fairly washed out. The doorway is plain and lintelled, its jambs much broken.

Drumcliff, Co. Clare

A rural graveyard 4km north-west of Ennis; follow the road to Corrofin.

A sliced-through and virtually featureless lower half of a tower, built with well-selected and roughly shaped field stones and laid in semi-regular courses. The doorway, which was in the missing part of the tower, was reportedly round-arched and architraved.

Drumcliff, Co. Sligo

A graveyard 7km north of Sligo on the Sligo-Ballyshannon road.

This is a low ruin of a tower built of very irregularly coursed rubble. It has a lintelled doorway and window.

Drumlane, Co. Cavan

A rural graveyard 1km south of Milltown; follow the Belturbet-Killeshandra road.

This is the lower half of a very fine tower, expertly built with irregularly coursed and well-tooled stone, cut as semi-ashlar and sometimes joggle-jointed. The upper third of the ruin has a different fabric – uncoursed rubble stone – which dates from the late Middle Ages and suggests that the top of the original tower had collapsed by then. There is a round-arched and architraved doorway (with three stones to the arch) in the lower part of the tower, and one window, with a monolithic arch, retrieved from the original tower and reset in the rubble part above the doorway. Two indistinct carvings of birds – a cock on the left and a hen on the right – are identified on the north side of the tower. A locally written late medieval recension of the life of Drumlane's founder, St Máedóc (St Aidan), describes him as blessing the site, laying out its ramparts and cemeteries, measuring and marking out its 'temples, churches and round towers', and organising its congregations and rituals.

Duleek, Co. Meath

A village graveyard, 8km south-west of Drogheda.

The scar of a now demolished Round Tower is visible in the north wall of the tower at the west end of St Mary's abbey church. It had been incorporated in the tower in the 1500s (see Lusk below for a parallel). The nature of the scar suggests the tower either leaned to the north or, more likely, that its circumference decreased as its ascended.

Dysert O'Dea, Co. Clare
A rural graveyard, 3km south of Corrofin; follow the road to Ennis.

As at neighbouring Drumcliff, half of this tower survives and that half is sliced through to reveal the simple interior of the drum. Here, though, the doorway, which is wide and round-arched. The stones are irregularly coursed, with some joggling, and long, flat stones predominate, particularly low down in the tower. The tower's most distinctive feature is a set-back (or ledge) which reduces its external diameter by about 50cm immediately above the doorway, giving the tower an upturned telescope affect. There is a late medieval ogee-headed window high up in the remaining portion.

Dysert Oenghusa, Co. Limerick
An open-land site 3km west of Croom; follow the road to Ballingarry.

This tower stands to more than half its original height. Constructed of local limestone which is irregularly coursed in the lower parts of the ruin but more regular higher up. The tower's most striking feature is its pronounced batter or taper. The doorway is round-arched in sandstone, and has a concave architrave filled with pellets where it turns around the arch. The windows, which mix round-arched, angle-headed and lintelled forms, are also in sandstone.

Faughart, Co. Louth
A rural graveyard 5km north of Dundalk; follow the old Dundalk-Newry road.

This is a problematic monument. A circle of stones has the correct circumference for a Round Tower, and the offset at the base is consistent with this identification, but the cross base in the centre of the ring suggests that this was an altar or a platform-base for the High Cross.

Fertagh, Co. Kilkenny
A rural graveyard 3km north of Johnstown; the tower is visible from the Durrow-Cashel road.

This is a very fine tower with an elegant batter or taper which is complete to cornice level. Its fabric is of small, squared-off blocks of local stone, neatly coursed. The original doorway is gone, replaced by infill during the repairs carried out in 1879-80. The windows are a mixture of lintelled and angle-headed.

Glendalough, Co. Wicklow

A famous site in the Wicklow mountains, well signposted; access to the monuments is free, but the heritage centre has an entrance fee.

Ireland's best-known Round Tower, this is now a complete building, its top having been reconstructed from fallen masonry in 1876. Its fabric is local mica-schist, laid in courses which are as regular as the material allows. Its doorway, which is monolithic and round-arched, is of granite. The windows are all lintelled.

Inis Cealtra, Co. Clare

An uninhabited island at the south end of Lough Derg. Access to the island is by private hire boat from Mountshannon.

A very fine tower which is complete to several metres below the bell-storey. Its masonry is irregularly coursed with stones of consistent size throughout but with larger stones at the bottom. The doorway is round-arched. The windows are all small lintelled openings apart from one large angle-headed window at the floor level above the doorway; Roscrea is a parallel for this arrangement. Excavations by the late Liam de Paor, still to be published, revealed postholes in the ground below the doorway, indicating a wooden structure giving access to the doorway.

Inishkeen, Co. Monaghan

A village graveyard 10km north-east of Carrickmacross; follow the Carrickmacross-Dundalk road.

This is a truncated tower of squared-off limestone blocks, roughly coursed. The lintelled doorway, like the rest of the tower, is much repaired.

Kells, Co. Meath

A graveyard in the centre of town.

This is a virtually complete tower: it stands to bell-storey height. It was built with local limestone, crudely squared off, fairly regularly coursed, and with many spalls. The sandstone doorway with its denuded figure sculpture (one, probably two, heads flanking the jambs) is probably a replacement of an original doorway. The windows are lintelled except at bell-storey level where there are five angle-headed windows.

Kilbennan, Co. Galway

A village graveyard 4km north-west of Tuam on the Tuam-Kilmaine road.

Half a tower remains here, built of well-squared blocks, joggle-jointed sometimes and irregularly coursed. The doorway is round-arched and in sandstone.
There are no surviving windows in the remaining portion.

Kilcoona, Co. Galway

A rural graveyard 6km south-east of Headford on the Headford-Galway road.

The base remains of a once-fine tower, made of well-squared limestone blocks
laid in regular courses and sometimes joggle-jointed.

Kildare, Co. Kildare

*The grounds of Kildare Cathedral in the centre of town. There is seasonal access to
the tower's interior.*

A complete tower except that its cap was replaced by a battlemented parapet
in the late Middle Ages. The base of the tower, to a height of about three
metres, which is just below the level of the doorway, is of well-coursed,
squared-off granite; it gives the impression, and probably falsely so, that the
main bulk of the tower that we see today is constructed on the foundation of
an older, better-built, tower. The tower upwards from this base is of local limestone, very irregularly coursed and with many small inserts of granite and sandstone. The tower's principal feature is the doorway, a pedimented Romanesque
doorway of the mid-twelfth century. Coins of this period were found under
the tower when excavations were carried out in 1843, and may have been
deposited there deliberately at the time of its construction.

Kilkenny, Co. Kilkenny

*The grounds of St Canice's Cathedral in the city. There is seasonal access to the
tower's interior.*

A complete tower except for its cap, replaced by a battlemented parapet in the
late Middle Ages. Built of local stone which is neatly coursed and dressed to
the curve, it has an elegant and consistent batter from bottom to top. The
doorway is round-arched, but the windows are all lintelled. The bell-storey has
six windows like that at Kilmacduagh.

Killala, Co. Mayo
The centre of the village, itself 12km north-west of Ballina.

This is a very fine and well-preserved tower of irregularly coursed limestone dressed to the curve. Large stones are used in the construction of its lower part, and spalls are used throughout. The doorway has a sandstone round-arch; the windows are all lintelled except at bell-storey level.

Killeany, Co. Galway
A rural site at the east end of Inishmore (Aran Islands). The island is accessible by boat (mainly from Rossaveal) and air (Inveran).

A stump of a Round Tower of well-squared limestone blocks, fairly regularly coursed with spalls. No features remain.

Killinaboy, Co. Clare
A rural graveyard 3km north-west of Corrofin on the Kilfenora road.

The featureless lower level remains of this tower, its irregular masonry prised open by weather and vegetation. Barrow suggested that a semi-monolithic arch built into the chancel of the church may have been the tower's doorway.

Kilmacduagh, Co. Galway
A rural site 4km south-west of Gort; follow the Gort-Corrofin road.

This is a magnificent tower, the tallest in Ireland. It leans markedly to one side, the result of being built with shallow foundations above graves. It owes its modern perfection as a monument to the careful and sensitive repair in 1878 of a breach on one side. The tower is of limestone construction, well squared and very well fitted together into irregular courses, especially in its lower parts. The doorway is semi-monolithic and round-arched, and the windows are all angle-headed on the outside and lintelled on the inside. The bell-storey has six windows rather than the usual four.

Kilmallock, Co. Limerick
Part of the medieval church of SS Peter and Paul in the village.

This tower is part of the west wall of a thirteenth-century collegiate church. Its lower part, from ground level to a height of just over two metres, seems to be of early medieval date and to have been a Round Tower; the remainder, which rises to a battlemented parapet about seventeen metres up, is later medieval. The original tower fabric is of local limestone, very irregularly coursed.

Kilree, Co. Kilkenny
A rural graveyard 2km south of Kells, itself 13km south of Kilkenny.

Another almost complete tower in the Kilkenny area, this, like the tower at Kilkenny itself, lacks only its original cap; in its place there is a late medieval battlemented parapet. It is built of local stone, squared off and irregularly coursed. It rises off a square plinth, like the truncated tower at Aghaviller. The doorway is monolithic and round-arched with an architrave.

Kinneigh, Co. Cork
A village graveyard 4km north-west of Enniskean; follow the Bandon-Dunmanway road.

A curious tower, distinguished by having a hexagonal base which gives it the appearance of a nineteenth-century mineworks chimney. The tower is built of slate, laid in fairly good horizontal courses and well squared, especially at the quoins of the base. The doorway, which is lintelled, is in one of the faces of the base rather than in the drum. The drum, which has a marked batter, rises to perhaps more than half its original height; its uppermost part dates from the insertion of a bell in the mid-1800s. The windows are all lintelled. The entrance storey had a flagstone floor.

Liathmore, Co. Tipperary
Open country on the east side of the Dublin-Cork road about 22km to the north-east of Cashel and close to the turn for Thurles; signposted.

The tidied-up foundation of a tower revealed in excavations over thirty years ago.

Lusk, Co. Dublin
A village graveyard 20km north of Dublin.

This virtually complete Round Tower – it lacks only its cap – has been incorporated into a fifteenth-century bell-tower, and its basic shape and plan, though not its bulk, replicated by three other cylindrical towers at the other corners. It is a well-built tower of local stone with good curvature to the stones. The doorway is now less than a metre above ground level but original ground level is at least two metres below. The windows in the drum are all lintelled.

Maghera, Co. Down
Outside a village graveyard 3km north of Newcastle; follow the Newcastle-Castlewellan road.

The stump of a tower of relatively little architectural interest. Its fabric is largely comprised of granite boulders uncoursed and packed around with small stones. There is a large opening in one side of it, which may be where the doorway was. The tower was repaired in the 1870s and conserved in the 1970s.

Meelick, Co. Mayo
A rural graveyard 5km south-west of Swinford; follow the Swinford-Castlebar road.

Most of this tower survives: it is truncated just below the level of its bell-storey. It is built of sandstone laid in good, regular, courses, highlighted by unobtrusive repointing in the later 1800s. The doorway is round-arched, the windows a combination of lintelled and angle-headed forms. There is a stone vault halfway up the interior of the tower.

Monasterboice, Co. Louth
A rural site 8km north of Drogheda; follow the Drogheda-Dundalk road.

This is a nearly complete tower with a broken top which may have been caused by a fire in 1097. Built of local slate in irregular courses with many spalls; the openings are of sandstone. The doorway is round-arched with a slightly more elaborate architrave than is usually found. The windows are lintelled apart from an angle-headed window directly above the doorway.

Nendrum, Co. Down
Island Mahee in Strangford Lough, 9km south-east of Comber. Access to the island is by causeway.

Only the lower, and featureless, part remains of this tower, and this is largely a product of early twentieth-century restoration. Its small diameter suggests the original tower was not especially lofty.

Old Kilcullen, Co. Kildare

A rural graveyard on a hill-top, 14km south-west of Naas; follow the Naas-Carlow road.

This is a truncated Round Tower of local slate, largely uncoursed. It was apparently quite a low tower – not much higher than it stands today – when fairly complete in the 1700s. The doorway is round-arched and there is one small lintelled window.

Oran, Co. Roscommon

On the opposite side of the road from a rural graveyard, 12km north-west of Roscommon; follow the Roscommon-Castlerea road.

This is the base of a large and exceptionally well-built tower; it was constructed of long slabs of local limestone, neatly squared-off and coursed.

Oughterard, Co. Kildare

A rural graveyard, on a hill-top, 10km north-east of Naas; follow the Dublin-Naas dual-carriageway and turn for Castlewarden.

A truncated tower which, with its fabric of uncoursed local shale, has an appropriately splintered appearance. Photographs prior to repointing in the late 1970s show a pattern of putlog (scaffold) stone spiralling upwards in a clockwise direction, which was an unconventional building technique in the early Middle Ages. The doorway is round-arched and of granite. The upper part of the ruined tower may be a late medieval rebuilding.

Ram's Island, Co. Antrim

An uninhabited, tree-covered island 2km offshore in east central Lough Neagh. Access by private-hire boat from Kinnigo Marina, Oxford Island.

A virtually featureless (and, apparently, thin-walled) tower, this stands to perhaps half its original height. It was built with largely undressed field stones and small boulders laid in irregular courses. It has a striking batter or taper. A filled-in breach at ground level marks a post-medieval door opening; the original upper-level doorway is now marked by a gap in the wall.

Rathmichael, Co. Dublin

A rural graveyard, 2km east of Shankill, itself 3km north of Bray.

The featureless stump of a tower of mixed granite and limestone, roughly coursed with spalls.

Rattoo, Co. Kerry

Outside a rural graveyard 1km south-east of Ballyduff, itself on the Ballybunion-Tralee road.

This is among the most perfect of the surviving towers; it is largely intact from the Middle Ages but the cap has been reset. Its fabric is largely of local sandstone, neatly if slightly irregularly coursed with spalls. The doorway is round-arched with an architrave. There is a very slight and barely visible moulding featuring small scrolls running concentrically with the architrave on the arch stones. Curiously, the only window other than at bell-storey level is a small angle-headed window two-thirds up the tower above the doorway. A sheela-na-gig with accompanying pellet ornament embellishes one of the bell-storey windows.

Roscam, Co. Galway

A rural graveyard, 6km east of Galway on the old Galway-Oranmore road.

This tower survives to less than half its original height; its present top is late medieval, suggesting that the tower was a ruin by the fifteenth century. The tower is built of local limestone, nicely squared and arranged in fairly regular courses. The drum is ringed by putlog (scaffolding) holes. The doorway is lintelled. The window above it – the only other opening in the tower – is also lintelled.

Roscrea, Co. Tipperary

A roadside site in the centre of town.

This is a fine tower built of local limestone which is tidily squared off and laid in neat horizontal courses. Its doorway is round-arched with an architrave. There is a large, angle-headed window at the next floor level up, and this bears a carving of a single-masted ship. The tower's height was allegedly lowered in the eighteenth century.

St Mullins, Co. Carlow

A graveyard in the small cul-de-sac village of St Mullins, located 12km south of Borris and 2km off the Borris to New Ross road.

Only the basal five courses remain of a well-built tower. The stones are laid in good horizontal courses and are nicely dressed to the curve of the wall.

Scattery Island, Co. Clare

An uninhabited island in the Shannon estuary, close to Kilrush. Access to the island is by boat from Cappagh pier, 1km south of Kilrush.

This is an odd tower which has excited much comment over the years. It stands to its full height minus (apparently) the top of its cap; a tradition (surely unreliable) that the cap was left unfinished has been recorded. The tower cylinder tapers markedly but with very uneven curvature – it's bumpy, in other words – from base to cap. The masonry is irregularly coursed sandstone that uses stones of consistent size throughout, with some courses of large interspersed. The windows are all lintelled and are all very small, even at the bell-storey. The most curious feature is its doorway, which is at ground level and has a form of corbelled arch.

Seir Kieran, Co. Offaly

A rural graveyard in Clareen, 13km north of Roscrea on the Roscrea-Tullamore road

This is the base of a tower of local limestone, fairly regularly coursed. It is featureless, but a bullaun stone – a stone with a circular depression created and deepened by grinding with another, smaller, stone – is incorporated into the modern entrance in it.

Swords, Co. Dublin

A village graveyard in a satellite town of modern Dublin, which is 13km to the south.

This tower is almost complete; its bell-storey is a later, probably seventeenth-century, replacement of the original. Built with undressed local limestone rubble and with relatively little coursing, it is a rather unattractive, crumbly-looking tower. Its doorway is lintelled, as are the surviving windows. The second floor inside had a flagstone floor, corbelled out of the wall.

Taghadoe, Co. Kildare

A rural graveyard, 3km south of Maynooth on the Maynooth-Straffan road.

About half remains of a very fine tower of local limestone, neatly coursed and dressed to the curve of the wall. The doorway is round-arched and architraved, and made in granite; its east jamb is of limestone and carries no architrave, so it is probably well-disguised later repair work. Above the keystone of the arch is a defaced head. The surviving windows are lintelled.

Timahoe, Co. Laois

A village graveyard, 10km south-east of Portlaoise on the Portlaoise-Castlecomer road.

This is now a complete Round Tower, its cap having been repaired in the early 1880s. Like the tower at Kildare, its basal part, to a height of about three metres and just below the level of the doorway, is of a different material (in this case sandstone) from the remainder of the tower (which is again of local limestone). The stones throughout are moderately well coursed, although the horizontal lines break down as the tower rises. The tower's principal feature is its Romanesque doorway of mid-twelfth-century date. The windows are a mixture of angle-headed, lintelled and round-arched types; an angle-headed window at the floor level above the doorway is especially elaborate, essentially repeating the design of sculpture on the doorway.

Tory Island, Co. Donegal

A roadside site in West Town village. Weather-dependent access to the island is by boat from Magheraroarty pier on Ballynass Bay.

This is a low tower, with sufficient remaining of its upper part to indicate that it was never very tall. The fabric is comprised of small granite boulders, largely uncoursed but with many spalls giving it horizontal lines. The doorway is round-arched with, uniquely, small flat stones forming the arch. There is also a small lintelled window. A large breach on one side of the tower was repaired in 1879-80 in a fashion different from, but in keeping with, the original fabric. There was originally a vault over the second (penultimate) floor.

Tullaherin, Co. Kilkenny
A rural graveyard, 2km west of Dungarvan; follow the Carlow-Waterford road.

A fine tower which stands to near its original height, as with the towers of Kilree and Kilkenny within its locality, the original bell-storey and cap are missing, replaced in the late Middle Ages with a new, six-windowed, bell-storey (like at the tower in Clonmacnoise) and a battlemented parapet. Its fabric is comprised of neatly squared-off blocks in regular courses of consistent size from bottom to top. The original doorway, probably round-arched, has gone, its space filled in with a pedestal of stone. The windows are lintelled.

Turlough, Co. Mayo
A rural graveyard 6km east of Castlebar on the Castlebar-Swinford road.

This is a relatively short but complete tower with a striking batter or taper. It is built of sandstone laid in fairly regular courses. The doorway, which is blocked, is round-arched; the windows are lintelled in the tower drum but angle-headed in the bell-storey. A ground-level doorway was created in the tower in the eighteenth-century but was blocked when the tower was repaired in the 1880s.

List of abbreviations

The annals are published and the abbreviations for these are as follows:

AClon D. Murphy (ed.), *The Annals of Clonmacnoise, being Annals of Ireland from the Earliest Period to A.D. 1408* (Dublin 1896).

AFM J. O'Donovan (ed. & trans.), *Annala Rioghachta Éireann; Annals of the Kingdom of Ireland by the Four Masters from the Earliest Period to the Year 1616*. 7 vols (Dublin 1851).

AI S. Mac Airt (ed. & trans.), *The Annals of Innisfallen (MS Rawlinson B.503)* (Dublin 1951).

ALC W.M. Hennessy (ed. & trans.), *The Annals of Lough Cé* (London 1871).

AT W. Stokes (ed.), 'The Annals of Tigernach', *Revue Celtique* xvi-xviii (1895-7).

AU S. Mac Airt & G. Mac Niocaill (eds), *Annals of Ulster (to A.D. 1131)* (Dublin 1983).

CS W.M. Hennessy (ed.), *Chronicon Scotorum, a Chronicle of Irish Affairs, from the Earliest Times to A.D. 1135* (London 1886).

MIA S. Ó hInnse (ed.), *Miscellaneous Irish Annals AD 1114-1437* (Dublin 1947).

Further reading

Selected references arranged chronologically

G. Petrie, *The Ecclesiastical Architecture of Ireland anterior to the Anglo-Norman Invasion,
comprising an essay on the Origin and Uses of Round Towers of Ireland*, Dublin 1845,
reprinted Dublin 1970.

M. Stokes, *The Early Christian Architecture of Ireland*, London 1875.

R.R. Brash, *The Ecclesiastical Architecture of Ireland*, Dublin 1875.

Lord Dunraven, *Notes on Irish Architecture*, 2 vols, London 1875-77.

A. Champneys, *Irish Ecclesiastical Architecture*, London 1910.

H.G. Leask, *Irish Churches and Monastic Buildings. I. The Early Phases and the Romanesque*,
Dundalk 1955.

A. Gwynn & N.D. Hadcock, *Medieval Religious Houses: Ireland*, London 1970.

C.A.R. Radford, 'The earliest Irish churches', *Ulster Journal of Archaeology*, 3rd series, 40
(1977), pp.1-11.

G.L. Barrow, *The Round Towers of Ireland*, Dublin 1979.

C. Bourke, 'Early Irish hand-bells', *Journal of the Royal Society of Antiquaries of Ireland* 110
(1980), pp.52-66.

E. Rynne, 'The Round Towers of Ireland: a review article', *North Munster Antiquarian
Journal* 22 (1980), pp.27-32.

P. Harbison, 'Early Irish churches', in H. Löwe (ed), *Die Iren und Europa im früheren
Mittelalter*, Stuttgart 1982, pp.618-29.

C. Doherty, 'The basilica in early Ireland', *Peritia* 3 (1984), pp.303-15.

Hamlin, 'The study of early Irish churches', in P. Ní Chatháin & M. Richter (eds),
Irland und Europa: Die Kirche im Frühmittelalter/Ireland and Europe: the Early Church,
Stuttgart 1984, pp.117–26.

M. Hare with A. Hamlin, 'The study of early church architecture in Ireland: an Anglo-
Saxon viewpoint, with an appendix on documentary evidence for round towers', in
L.A.S. Butler & R.K. Morris (eds), *The Anglo-Saxon Church*, London 1986,
pp.131-45.

M. Herity, 'The Antiquity of *an Turas* (the Pilgrimage Round) in Ireland', in A. Lehner & W. Berschin (eds), *Lateinische Kultur im VIII Jahrhundert*, St Ottilien 1989, pp.95-143.

P. Harbison, *Pilgrimage in Ireland: the Monuments and the People*, London and Syracuse 1992.

P. Harbison, *Guide to the National and Historic Monuments of Ireland*, Dublin 1992.

M. Herity, 'The forms of the tomb-shrine of the founder saint in Ireland', in R.M. Spearman & J. Higgitt (eds), *The Age of Migrating Ideas*, Stroud 1993, pp.188-95.

H. McDonnell, 'Margaret Stokes and the Irish Round Tower: a reappraisal', *Ulster Journal of Archaeology*, 3rd series, 47 (1994), pp.40-50.

J. Leerssen, *Remembrance and Imagination. Patterns in the Historical and Literary Representation of Ireland in the Nineteenth Century*, Cork 1996, esp. pp.68-156.

T. O'Keeffe, 'Architectural traditions of the early medieval church in Munster', in M.A. Monk & J. Sheehan (eds), *Early Medieval Munster*, Cork 1998, pp.112-24.

B. Lalor, *The Irish Round Tower*, Cork 1999.

S. O'Reilly, 'Birth of a nation's symbol: the revival of Ireland's Round Towers', *Irish Arts Review Yearbook* 15 (1999), pp.27-33.

Manning, 'References to church buildings in the annals', in A. Smyth (ed), *Seanchas. Studies in Early and Medieval Irish Archaeology, History and Literature in Honour of Francis J. Byrne*, Dublin 2000, pp.37-52.

R. Stalley, *Irish Round Towers*, Dublin 2000.

T. O'Keeffe, 'Form and content in pre-Romanesque architecture in Ireland', *European Symposium of Teachers of Medieval Archaeology* 4 (2001), pp.65-83.

R. Stalley, 'Sex, symbol, and myth: some observations on the Irish Round Towers', in C. Hourihane (ed), *From Ireland Coming. Irish Art from the Early Christian to the Late Gothic Period and its European Context*, Princeton 2001, pp.27-48.

T. O'Keeffe, *Romanesque Ireland. Architecture and Ideology in the Twelfth Century*, Dublin 2003.

Index to sites

If you are interested in purchasing
other books published by Tempus, or in case you have
difficulty finding any Tempus books in your local bookshop,
you can also place orders directly through our website

www.tempus-publishing.com

or from

BOOKPOST
Freepost, PO Box 29,
Douglas, Isle of Man
IM99 1BQ
Tel 01624 836000
email bookshop@enterprise.net